Bitcoin

Blueprint

UNRAVELING THE REVOLUTIONARY
DIGITAL CURRENCY

Harrison Stratton

Table of Contents

Introduction

Welcome to "Bitcoin Blueprint: Unraveling the Revolutionary Digital Currency." We go on an insightful exploration of the world of Bitcoin in this e-book, a revolutionary digital currency that has captivated the interest of millions of people worldwide. We will examine the transformative power of Bitcoin and its ability to revolutionize the financial landscape as we delve into the nuances of this revolutionary technology.

In recent years, Bitcoin has become a representation of financial innovation, decentralization, and individual sovereignty. In 2008, the mysterious persona known only as Satoshi Nakamoto created Bitcoin, which popularized the idea of a digital money that runs decentralized, peer-to-peer, and resistant to censorship. Because of its decentralized structure and innovative blockchain technology have opened up a variety of opportunities that go against established financial norms.

We will start by setting the stage in this e-book by giving a general review of traditional currencies and their constraints on our financial systems. Comprehending these constraints is crucial to appreciate the importance of Bitcoin's rise and its potential to influence international banking significantly.

We will go deeply into the blockchain, the underlying technology of Bitcoin. In addition to making Bitcoin safe, this decentralized and unchangeable ledger has created numerous alternative cryptocurrencies, each with their own special characteristics and possible applications.

We will dissect the workings of Bitcoin transactions as we explore, going through the functions of wallets, public and private keys, and the mining procedure that secures and verifies the network. We will also cover Bitcoin's turbulent rise to notoriety, from its relative obscurity in the early days to its mainstreaming as a topic in financial conversations.

We will address the legal and regulatory issues surrounding Bitcoin as we work through the intricacies of its rise. Globally, governments and financial institutions have struggled with dealing with this disruptive technology, which has resulted in various legislative reactions that have influenced the cryptocurrency market.

Of course, the urgent issue of Bitcoin's environmental impact must be brought up in any conversation regarding the technology. We will look at how much energy is used in Bitcoin mining and investigate the industry's efforts to adopt sustainable methods.

Furthermore, this e-book will investigate the larger cryptocurrency ecosystem and go beyond Bitcoin itself. The wide range of cryptocurrencies known as altcoins, which are different from

Bitcoin, have given rise to creative initiatives and applications highlighting blockchain technology's revolutionary possibilities.

The world of digital currencies is not without its difficulties, though. We will examine the security threats associated with Bitcoin and the best ways for consumers to protect their holdings from harm.

Finally, we will look ahead and examine prospective advancements and the possible effects of Bitcoin on the world financial scene. Will Bitcoin overcome challenges that impede its development or will it become a necessary component of our daily lives, revolutionizing how we handle money?

Ultimately, the goal of "Bitcoin Blueprint: Unraveling the Revolutionary Digital Currency" is to teach you a thorough grasp of both the revolutionary potential of Bitcoin and its ramifications for the financial industry going forward. This e-book provides insights into the decentralized and transformational potential of Bitcoin, which is reshaping the financial world as we know it, whether you are a novice or an experienced enthusiast. So let's set off on this fascinating adventure together to learn about the fascinating world of Bitcoin.

Chapter I
Understanding Bitcoin

Overview of Bitcoin

Bitcoin, the revolutionary digital currency, has captured the world's attention and disrupted traditional financial systems since its inception in 2008. The Bitcoin system, which runs on a decentralized network without being governed by a central authority, was developed by an unidentified individual known only as Satoshi Nakamoto. The basic elements of Bitcoin will be covered in this overview, along with its core technology, the blockchain, special features, and the factors driving its rising popularity.

Fundamentally, Bitcoin is a decentralized virtual currency that eliminates the requirement for intermediaries like banks and enables users to conduct safe, open transactions. As a decentralized network of computers called nodes jointly maintain the blockchain, Bitcoin transactions are validated and recorded by these nodes as opposed to a central authority like a government or financial institution.

The public ledger known as the blockchain, which forms the basis of Bitcoin, keeps track of every transaction ever made with the virtual currency. Peer-to-peer networking allows it to function and guarantees that all users have access to the same data, increasing security and transparency. A continuous data chain is created by grouping transactions into blocks and connecting them chronologically. This structure makes the blockchain immutable, as altering any past transaction would require changing all subsequent blocks, which is computationally infeasible and highly secure.

The restricted quantity of Bitcoin is one of its main characteristics. In contrast to conventional fiat currencies, which are unlimited in quantity, the total quantity of Bitcoin is limited to 21 million coins. This scarcity is hardcoded into the protocol, and as a result, Bitcoin is often compared to precious metals like gold, with proponents arguing that it can serve as a store of value and a hedge against inflation.

Users require a digital wallet in order to access and manage Bitcoin. A wallet is made up of two cryptographic keys: a private key that is used to access the funds and sign transactions, and a public key that acts as an address to receive Bitcoin. When working with cryptocurrencies, security is crucial since misplacing a private key might result in irreversible loss of access to the linked funds.

Bitcoin transactions are propagated through the network and validated by miners. Mining is the process by which new transactions are added to the blockchain, and new Bitcoins are minted. Miners compete to solve challenging mathematical puzzles; the first to do so successfully adds the next block to the blockchain and receives transaction fees and freshly minted Bitcoins as payment.

The decentralized nature of Bitcoin and the consensus mechanism through mining ensure that the network is resilient and censorship-resistant. Transactions cannot be easily blocked or reversed, making it a popular choice for individuals as well as businesses seeking financial autonomy and privacy.

Significant price volatility has marked Bitcoin's journey from obscurity to prominence. In its early years, Bitcoin was worth just a fraction of a cent, but over time, its value skyrocketed, attracting the attention of investors and speculators. This volatility has sparked debates about its role as a currency versus a speculative asset, but it has also brought mainstream awareness to the broader potential of blockchain technology.

Furthermore, Bitcoin's use cases have expanded beyond simple peer-to-peer transactions. It provides a quicker and less expensive option to conventional banking systems for remittances and cross-border payments. Furthermore, some see Bitcoin as a possible "digital gold," a store of value that might guard against inflation and unstable economies.

As Bitcoin gained popularity, it also faced regulatory scrutiny from various governments and financial authorities worldwide. Because Bitcoin is decentralized and pseudonymous, there are worries that it could be used for illicit purposes like tax evasion and money laundering. Consequently, different countries have adopted varying regulatory approaches, ranging from outright bans to more accommodating frameworks.

In conclusion, Bitcoin is a groundbreaking digital currency that has the potential to reshape the financial landscape. Its decentralized nature, secured by the blockchain, offers a new vision for a trustless and transparent financial system. As the world continues grappling with this disruptive technology's implications, Bitcoin's journey is far from over. Its impact on global finance, economics, and society is still unfolding, and its future remains an intriguing frontier in digital innovation.

Importance and impact of Bitcoin on the financial landscape

Bitcoin, the revolutionary digital currency introduced by Satoshi Nakamoto in 2008, has emerged as a significant disruptor in the financial landscape. Its decentralized and peer-to-peer nature challenges the traditional financial system's reliance on central authorities and intermediaries. This section explores the importance and impact of Bitcoin on the financial landscape, covering its role in financial inclusion, remittances, cross-border payments, the store of value, hedging against inflation, and its potential to reshape global finance.

One of the key aspects of Bitcoin's importance lies in its potential to promote financial inclusion. In many parts of the world, conventional banking services are limited or inaccessible, leaving millions of people without access to essential financial tools. Bitcoin offers an alternative by enabling anyone with an internet connection to make a digital wallet and participate in the global economy. This is especially valuable in regions with unstable or inflation-prone fiat currencies, where people may seek refuge in

Bitcoin to protect their wealth and conduct transactions securely and independently.

Furthermore, Bitcoin has emerged as an attractive option for remittances and cross-border payments. Traditional remittance services often involve high fees and lengthy processing times, particularly for transactions involving different currencies. Bitcoin's ability to facilitate near-instantaneous cross-border transactions at a fraction of the cost of traditional methods has made it an appealing choice for individuals and businesses seeking to streamline their international financial activities.

Another significant impact of Bitcoin lies in its role as a store of value. As a limited-supply digital currency, Bitcoin's scarcity has drawn comparisons to precious metals like gold. Some investors and enthusiasts view Bitcoin as a modern digital gold, asserting that its fixed supply and decentralized nature make it an attractive asset for preserving wealth. During times of economic uncertainty, political instability, or currency devaluation, Bitcoin has gained traction as a potential safe haven asset, providing a level of financial security beyond traditional fiat currencies.

Furthermore, Bitcoin has shown its potential as a hedge against inflation. Inflation, driven by factors like central bank policies and economic fluctuations, erodes the purchasing power of fiat currencies over time. As a deflationary asset, Bitcoin's supply is limited, which can result in an increased demand and potential price appreciation over time. Investors seeking protection against inflation may turn to Bitcoin to preserve the value of their wealth, especially in times of economic turbulence.

Moreover, Bitcoin's impact on the financial landscape extends beyond individual use cases. It has sparked a wave of innovation in the financial technology sector, with various cryptocurrency exchanges, investment platforms, and blockchain-based financial products emerging. The rise of decentralized finance (DeFi) platforms, which leverage smart contracts to provide financial services without traditional intermediaries, exemplifies how Bitcoin's underlying blockchain technology has influenced the evolution of financial systems.

However, Bitcoin's increasing prominence has not been without challenges. Its volatility has raised concerns about its suitability as a reliable means of exchange. Critics argue that frequent price fluctuations make it impractical for everyday transactions, as the value of goods and services could vary significantly over short periods. Moreover, scalability issues have led to slower transaction processing times and higher fees during peak periods, impacting Bitcoin's utility for microtransactions.

Regulatory scrutiny has also been a significant factor in Bitcoin's impact on the financial landscape. Governments and financial institutions worldwide have grappled with how to address this disruptive technology. While some countries have embraced cryptocurrencies and blockchain technology, others have imposed strict regulations or outright bans, creating a patchwork of regulatory landscapes that can impact Bitcoin's adoption and use on a global scale.

Despite these challenges, the importance and impact of Bitcoin on the financial landscape are undeniable. Its disruptive potential has forced traditional financial institutions to take notice and explore the integration of blockchain technology into their operations. Major companies and institutional investors have also entered the space, signaling growing mainstream acceptance of cryptocurrencies as a legitimate asset class.

In conclusion, Bitcoin's emergence as a revolutionary digital currency has significantly impacted the financial landscape. From promoting financial inclusion to offering an alternative for cross-border payments, acting as a store of value, and potentially hedging against inflation, Bitcoin has opened up new opportunities for individuals as well as businesses worldwide. Its underlying blockchain technology has sparked innovation and reshaped the fintech sector. However, challenges related to volatility, scalability, and regulatory uncertainty remain. As the financial world continues to evolve, Bitcoin's importance as a disruptive force and its impact on the global financial landscape will continue to be a topic of great interest and exploration.

Chapter II
Understanding Traditional Currencies and Money Systems

Evolution of money: From barter to fiat currencies

As a medium of exchange, money has played a central role in human civilization, facilitating trade, commerce, and economic growth. The evolution of money is a fascinating journey that reflects the development of human societies and their need for efficient and reliable transaction methods. This section explores the historical progression of money, from primitive barter systems to modern nation-states' adoption of fiat currencies, revealing the fundamental shifts in economic structures and the profound impact of monetary innovations on human society.

The barter system, in which products and services were directly traded for other goods and services, formed the foundation of the first commercial economy. This simple form of trade was prevalent in small, close-knit communities where individuals had personal relationships and clear knowledge of the value of various commodities. However, barter had inherent limitations, such as the double coincidence of wants, where two parties had to want each other's goods simultaneously, making exchanges cumbersome and inefficient.

To overcome the limitations of barter, societies transitioned to using commodity money. Commodity money consisted of objects with intrinsic value, such as precious metals like the gold and silver. These metals were valued for their rarity, durability, and divisibility, making them an ideal medium of exchange. Ancient civilizations, including the Greeks, Romans, and Mesopotamians, adopted commodity money to facilitate trade across more significant regions, reducing the reliance on barter and enabling the growth of complex economic systems.

As societies continued to evolve, the use of precious metals as commodity money became more widespread. Merchants and traders would carry gold and silver coins on their journeys, allowing them to conduct business in different regions with confidence in the value of their currency. The standardization of coinage, often with the ruler's or state's imprint, further enhanced trust and facilitated trade on a larger scale.

The next stage in the evolution of money came with the rise of representative money. This form of currency represented a claim on a commodity, such as gold or silver, stored securely by a trusted entity, such as a bank or government. Holders of these claims could exchange them for the underlying commodity upon request. Representative money provided greater convenience and security than carrying physical metals, as individuals could conduct transactions using paper notes or other instruments backed by the commodity's value.

One of the significant milestones in monetary history was the emergence of paper money. Paper money can be traced back to ancient China during the Tang Dynasty, where promissory notes were used as a form of currency. Paper money gained widespread acceptance as an alternative to commodity-backed money due to its portability and ease of use. As European societies embraced the concept of paper money, it enabled the growth of complex financial systems, leading to the establishment of the world's first central banks in the 17th century.

The 19th century marked a critical turning point in the evolution of money with the adoption of fiat currencies. Fiat money is currency that has value because a government or authority decrees it to be legal tender and accepts it for tax payments and other public obligations. Unlike commodity-backed money, fiat money has no intrinsic value and relies solely on the trust and confidence of the people using it. The transition to fiat currencies marked a significant departure from the historical reliance on tangible assets to back currency value.

The Bretton Woods Agreement accelerated the widespread adoption of fiat currencies in 1944, which established the U.S. dollar as the reserve currency of the world, linked to gold at a fixed rate. Under this system, other countries pegged their currencies to the U.S. dollar, indirectly linking their currencies to gold. However, this system eventually collapsed in 1971 when the United States abandoned the gold standard, resulting in the complete decoupling of fiat currencies from any physical commodity.

The era of fully fiat currencies ushered in a new chapter in the history of money, characterized by unprecedented monetary flexibility and the ability of governments to control the money supply. While this flexibility allowed central banks to implement monetary policies to stabilize economies and manage inflation, it also gave rise to concerns about currency devaluation and hyperinflation in some instances.

The digital age brought further transformations to the concept of money, leading to the development of digital currencies and cryptocurrencies. Digital currencies, like those used in online transactions and banking, are essentially electronic representations of fiat money. They exist only in digital form and can be transferred and used for transactions electronically.

Cryptocurrencies, conversely, are a revolutionary form of digital money operating on decentralized blockchain technology. Bitcoin, introduced in 2008, is the first and most well-known cryptocurrency. It allows for peer-to-peer transactions without intermediaries, offering a level of financial autonomy and security previously unseen in traditional banking systems.

As the world explores the potential of digital currencies and cryptocurrencies, the future of money remains subject to ongoing debates and discussions. While the evolution of money has brought about significant economic growth and financial innovation, it has also posed challenges related to financial stability, inequality, and the role of governments in managing monetary policies.

In conclusion, the evolution of money from barter to fiat currencies reflects the ingenuity and adaptability of human societies in finding efficient and reliable means of conducting trade and commerce. From the simple act of bartering goods to the complexity of fiat currencies backed by trust and decree, money has played a pivotal role in shaping economies and civilizations. The rise of digital currencies and cryptocurrencies in the modern era opens new possibilities and challenges for the future of money, emphasizing the need for thoughtful consideration of monetary systems that promote economic stability, financial inclusion, and sustainable growth.

How central banks control traditional currencies

Central banks are critical in controlling traditional currencies and influencing a nation's monetary policy. As the guardians of a country's economic stability and financial system, central banks employ various tools and mechanisms to manage money supply, interest rates, and overall economic growth. This section explores the methods and strategies central banks use to control traditional currencies, delving into the significance of monetary policy in ensuring price stability, promoting economic growth, and mitigating financial crises.

The primary tool at a central bank's disposal for controlling traditional currencies is manipulating interest rates. Central banks manipulate the monetary supply in the economy by purchasing or disposing of government securities through open market operations. The central bank buys government-issued securities from commercial banks in order to provide cash to the economy in an effort to boost economic activity and the money supply. This process reduces interest rates, making borrowing cheaper for businesses and individuals, thus stimulating spending and investment.

Conversely, when the central bank aims to curb inflation or prevent overheating in the economy, it may sell government securities to commercial banks, reducing the money supply and raising interest rates. Higher interest rates make borrowing more expensive, curbing spending and investment and controlling inflationary pressures. The manipulation of interest rates is a powerful tool used by central banks to regulate economic growth and maintain price stability.

Apart from interest rates, central banks also control traditional currencies through reserve requirements. Reserve requirements mandate that commercial banks must hold a certain percentage of their deposits as reserves at the central bank. By raising or lowering these reserve requirements, central banks can affect the amount of money that commercial banks can lend out to consumers and businesses.

When reserve requirements are raised, banks have less money available to lend, leading to reduced credit availability, higher interest rates, and decreased economic activity. Conversely, lowering reserve requirements boosts lending capacity, making credit more accessible and encouraging economic expansion.

Central banks use reserve requirements to ensure the banking system's stability and manage inflation and economic growth.

Moreover, central banks employ open market operations, buying and selling foreign currencies to impact exchange rates and stabilize their country's currency. When a central bank wants to strengthen its currency, it may buy foreign currencies, increasing demand for its domestic currency, and thereby driving up its value relative to other currencies. A stronger currency can benefit a nation's imports, making foreign goods cheaper for consumers and businesses.

Conversely, when a central bank wants to weaken its currency, it may sell foreign currencies, reducing demand for its domestic currency and driving down its value. A weaker currency can boost exports, making domestically produced goods more competitive in international markets. Central banks aim to support export-driven growth by managing exchange rates or protecting domestic industries from volatile currency fluctuations.

Central banks also utilize various direct lending facilities and discount rates to provide financial assistance to commercial banks during times of crisis or liquidity shortages. During economic downturns or financial crises, central banks can lend funds directly to commercial banks at a discount rate, allowing banks to access liquidity and continue their operations. These lending facilities act as a safety net for the banking system, preventing widespread bank failures and ensuring financial stability.

Furthermore, central banks use forward guidance and communication strategies to influence market expectations and guide economic behavior. By publicly announcing their future policy intentions, central banks can shape the public's expectations regarding interest rates, inflation, and economic growth. Positive forward guidance can encourage spending and investment, while negative direction can promote saving and financial prudence.

In addition to these traditional tools, central banks have also employed unconventional monetary policy measures to combat extraordinary economic challenges. Quantitative easing (QE) is an unconventional measure where central banks buy government bonds or any other financial assets from the open market to inject additional liquidity into the financial system. The aim is to reduce long-term interest rates, encourage lending, and stimulate economic growth during economic stagnation.

Central banks' use of monetary policy tools is not without limitations and risks. Excessive expansion of the money supply can lead to inflation, eroding the purchasing power of a nation's currency. Conversely, overly tight monetary policy can stifle economic growth and exacerbate recessions. Striking the right balance requires central banks to assess economic indicators carefully, consider future risks, and adopt data-driven decision-making processes.

Moreover, the effectiveness of central bank policies can be impacted by external factors beyond their control, such as global economic conditions, international trade dynamics, and geopolitical events. Central banks must navigate these complexities while remaining committed to their primary objectives of maintaining price stability, fostering sustainable economic growth, and safeguarding the financial system's stability.

In conclusion, central banks is crucial in controlling traditional currencies and shaping a nation's monetary policy. By manipulating interest rates, reserve requirements, exchange rates, and other monetary tools, central banks seek to maintain price stability, promote economic growth, and mitigate financial crises. As the guardians of a country's economic well-being, central banks continuously adapt their strategies and policies to respond to changing economic conditions and ensure the entire health and stability of the financial landscape.

Limitations and challenges of traditional money systems

Traditional money systems, based on physical currencies and managed by central authorities, have served as the backbone of global economies for centuries. While these systems have facilitated trade and commerce, they have limitations and challenges. This section explores the constraints and issues that traditional money systems face, including inflation, deflation, exchange rate volatility, financial crises, and the rise of digital currencies, shedding light on the need for continued innovation in monetary policy and financial infrastructure.

One of the primary limitations of traditional money systems is the challenge of managing inflation and deflation. Inflation is the sustained increase in the overall price level of goods and services, eroding the purchasing power of money over time. Central banks strive to maintain a stable inflation rate, often targeting an optimal level of around 2% to promote economic growth and prevent deflationary pressures.

Conversely, deflation is the opposite phenomenon, characterized by a decrease in the general price level. While deflation may benefit consumers as goods become cheaper, it can reduce spending and investment. Individuals may postpone purchases, anticipating further price declines, leading to decreased demand and economic slowdown.

Balancing inflation and deflation can be a delicate task for central banks. Excessive money supply expansion can lead to runaway inflation, while overly tight monetary policies exacerbate inflationary pressures. Striking the proper balance is essential for maintaining price stability and fostering sustainable economic growth.

Exchange rate volatility is another significant challenge traditional money systems face, particularly in a globalized world with complex trade relationships. Exchange rates, the relative values of one currency against another, can fluctuate significantly due to various factors, including interest rate differentials, trade imbalances, geopolitical events, and speculative trading.

Currency volatility can pose risks for international trade and investment, impacting exporters, importers, and investors. Sudden and drastic exchange rate fluctuations can lead to uncertainty and create difficulties in planning and budgeting for businesses operating across borders.

Financial crises represent a major limitation of traditional money systems, and history has witnessed numerous episodes of economic turmoil and instability. The 2008 global financial crisis is an evident reminder of how vulnerabilities in financial systems and the mismanagement of monetary policies can have far-reaching consequences.

Financial crises can result from a combination of factors, including excessive lending and borrowing, asset bubbles, inadequate regulatory oversight, and systemic risks. The aftermath of such crises can lead to severe economic recessions, widespread unemployment, and significant disruptions to the financial sector.

Furthermore, traditional money systems face challenges related to financial inclusion and access to banking services. In many parts of the world, particularly in developing economies, a substantial portion of the population remains unbanked or underbanked, lacking access to basic financial tools like bank accounts, credit, and insurance.

This lack of financial inclusion can hinder economic growth and perpetuate income inequality. It also limits individuals' ability to save, invest, and participate in the formal economy, leading to a reliance on cash-based transactions and informal financial services.

Another limitation is the dependency on physical cash and the associated costs and risks. Physical currency production, transportation, and security entail substantial expenses for governments and financial institutions. Counterfeiting and theft are persistent concerns, necessitating investments in anti-counterfeiting measures and security infrastructure.

Moreover, using physical cash can facilitate illicit activities, such as money laundering and tax evasion, as it allows for anonymous and untraceable transactions. As a result, combating financial crimes becomes more challenging in cash-intensive economies.

Traditional money systems have faced competition and disruption from digital currencies and cryptocurrencies in recent years. Digital payment systems, like mobile wallets and online banking, have gained popularity due to their convenience, speed, and cost-effectiveness. These technologies enable cashless transactions, reducing the reliance on physical currency.

Cryptocurrencies, led by Bitcoin and others, have introduced a decentralized and borderless form of money that operates independently of central authorities. While cryptocurrencies offer potential financial inclusion, security, and transparency benefits, they also pose challenges related to regulatory oversight, price volatility, and potential use in illicit activities.

Moreover, the rapid pace of technological advancement has led several countries to explore central bank digital currencies (CBDCs). CBDCs are digital representations of a nation's fiat currency provided and regulated by the central bank. These digital currencies promise greater efficiency, financial inclusion, and enhanced monetary policy tools. However, their implementation requires careful consideration of cybersecurity, privacy, and interoperability with existing financial systems.

In conclusion, traditional money systems have served as the backbone of global economies, enabling trade, commerce, and economic growth. However, they are not without limitations and challenges. Balancing inflation and deflation, managing exchange rate volatility, addressing financial crises, and promoting financial inclusion are among the pressing issues central banks and policymakers face.

Additionally, the rise of digital currencies and cryptocurrencies presents both opportunities and risks for the future of money. The ongoing digitization of financial systems and the exploration of CBDCs highlight the need for continued innovation and adaptability in monetary policy and financial infrastructure.

As societies evolve and technological advancements continue, addressing the limitations and challenges of traditional money systems will remain a complex and dynamic process. Striving for financial stability, fostering inclusive economic growth, and harnessing the potential of digital innovations will be paramount in shaping the future of global monetary systems.

Chapter III
Birth of Bitcoin

The mysterious Satoshi Nakamoto

The name "Satoshi Nakamoto" has become synonymous with the revolutionary concept of Bitcoin, the world's first decentralized cryptocurrency. Yet, behind this pseudonym lies an enigmatic figure whose true identity remains one of the most enduring mysteries in the world of technology and finance. This section delves into the fascinating tale of Satoshi Nakamoto, exploring the origins of Bitcoin, the clues to Nakamoto's identity, the impact of the mysterious creator's creation, and the enduring allure of anonymity in the digital age.

The whitepaper with a title of "Bitcoin: A Peer-to-Peer Electronic Cash System," written in October 2008 by a person or group going by the pseudonym Satoshi Nakamoto, is where Bitcoin got its beginnings. A decentralized digital currency that operates without middlemen or centralized authorities was described in the whitepaper. It introduced the revolutionary technology of blockchain, a distributed ledger that underpins Bitcoin, ensuring its security, transparency, and immutability.

As the Bitcoin software was released in January 2009, Satoshi Nakamoto engaged with early adopters, developers, and enthusiasts through online forums and email communications. However, Nakamoto consistently strongly preferred privacy, rarely revealing personal details. This anonymity raised curiosity and speculation about Nakamoto's true identity, sparking various theories and investigations.

Numerous individuals have been identified as possible candidates for Satoshi Nakamoto over the years, ranging from cryptographers and computer scientists to entrepreneurs and privacy advocates. Yet, each alleged Nakamoto claim has lacked definitive proof, leaving the true identity of the Bitcoin creator shrouded in uncertainty.

Some have theorized that Satoshi Nakamoto may be a single individual, while others propose that it could be a collective effort involving multiple individuals. The use of English language proficiency and the absence of any identifiable accent in Nakamoto's writing have led some to suggest that Nakamoto could be a native English speaker or a team with members from English-speaking countries.

Additionally, Nakamoto's activity patterns, including timestamps of messages and code contributions, have led researchers to speculate about possible time zones in which Nakamoto may have been located. However, these clues have not yielded any conclusive evidence about Nakamoto's identity.

The idea of anonymity in the creation of Bitcoin has sparked debates about its implications. While some argue that the mystery surrounding Nakamoto adds to the allure and intrigue of Bitcoin, others express concerns about the potential for an anonymous creator to influence the cryptocurrency's development and price movements.

Beyond Nakamoto's identity, the impact of Bitcoin and blockchain technology has been profound. Bitcoin has evolved from an obscure experiment to a global phenomenon, attracting investors, technologists, and governments worldwide. The advent of blockchain technology has inspired the development of thousands of other cryptocurrencies and innovative blockchain-based applications, ranging from decentralized finance (DeFi) platforms to non-fungible tokens (NFTs) and beyond.

The creation of Bitcoin has challenged the traditional financial system, prompting discussions about the role of central banks, the future of money, and financial inclusion. It has given rise to debates about the nature of money itself, with some viewing Bitcoin as digital gold and a potential hedge against inflation, while others remain skeptical of its long-term stability and utility as a currency.

Moreover, Bitcoin's journey has been marked by significant price volatility and speculative investment, leading to fervent enthusiasm among early adopters and periods of skepticism and regulatory scrutiny from governments and financial institutions.

As Bitcoin grows and evolves, the question of Nakamoto's identity remains unanswered. Some have argued that Nakamoto's mystery should be respected, as the decision to stay anonymous reflects a principled stance on privacy and individuality. Others believe that uncovering Nakamoto's identity could clarify Bitcoin's early development and establish a sense of accountability.

Despite the intrigue surrounding Nakamoto's identity, the impact of Bitcoin and blockchain technology extends far beyond the realm of its creator. The growing global interest in cryptocurrencies and blockchain has fueled research, innovation, and investment, shaping the future of finance and technology.

Moreover, the concept of an anonymous creator speaks to broader themes of privacy, autonomy, and decentralization that resonate in the digital age. As technology continues to shape human society, the question of anonymity versus transparency in creation and innovation will persist.

Whitepaper release and early development

The October 2008 publication of the Bitcoin whitepaper by an individual or group going by the pseudonym Satoshi Nakamoto signaled the start of a transformative journey that would completely change the financial and technological landscapes. This section delves into the historic whitepaper, the foundational principles of Bitcoin, the early development of the cryptocurrency, and the key milestones that shaped its growth into a global phenomenon.

The Bitcoin whitepaper, titled "Bitcoin: A Peer-to-Peer Electronic Cash System," presented a radical new concept - an autonomous virtual money operating on a peer-to-peer network, allowing for direct transactions between parties without intermediaries or central authorities. Nakamoto's vision for Bitcoin was rooted in solving the double-spending problem that hindered previous attempts to create digital cash systems. By leveraging cryptographic techniques and a distributed ledger called the blockchain, Nakamoto proposed a system that would prevent double-spending and ensure the security and transparency of transactions.

The whitepaper outlined the core components of Bitcoin's design. It introduced the mining concept, a process by which new transactions are validated and added to the blockchain. Miners would compete to solve complicated mathematical puzzles, and the first one to find a valid solution would have the right to add the next block to the chain and be rewarded with newly minted bitcoins. This proof-of-work mechanism was the backbone of Bitcoin's security, making it computationally infeasible for malicious actors to alter past transactions.

The whitepaper also introduced the concept of nodes, computers participating in the Bitcoin network, and highlighted the importance of decentralization in ensuring the system's integrity. By having multiple nodes verify and store copies of the blockchain, Bitcoin could resist censorship and attacks, offering a level of robustness not seen in traditional financial systems.

In January 2009, Nakamoto released the first version of the Bitcoin software, making it publicly available for anyone to use and participate in the network. The software allowed users to create digital wallets, generate cryptographic key pairs, and begin transacting with bitcoins. The initial period of Bitcoin's development was characterized by a small and passionate community of enthusiasts who were drawn to the technology's potential for financial sovereignty and privacy.

The early adopters of Bitcoin were primarily cypherpunks, cryptographers, and tech enthusiasts who appreciated the underlying principles of decentralization and cryptography. Transactions in the early days were relatively modest, involving niche communities and experimental use cases. A notable early transaction occurred when Nakamoto sent 10 bitcoins to Hal Finney, a prominent figure in the cypherpunk community, marking the first-ever Bitcoin transaction.

2010 Bitcoin gained wider attention when it was used for a real-world commercial transaction. Laszlo Hanyecz famously paid 10,000 bitcoins to another user in exchange for two pizzas, an event now celebrated annually as "Bitcoin Pizza Day." This transaction highlighted Bitcoin's potential as a medium of exchange, although few could have predicted the significant rise in the value of bitcoin that would follow.

As Bitcoin's user base and popularity grew, so did the demand for a more user-friendly way to access and transact with the cryptocurrency. Early Bitcoin wallets and exchanges emerged in response to this need, providing more accessible interfaces for users to interact with the network. These developments helped pave the way for Bitcoin's broader adoption and laid the groundwork for the subsequent explosion of cryptocurrency-related services.

One of the early challenges faced by the Bitcoin community was the perception of the cryptocurrency as a tool for illicit activities and a medium for facilitating illegal transactions. The decentralized and pseudonymous nature of Bitcoin raised concerns about its potential use in money laundering, tax evasion, and other criminal activities. However, research and analysis have shown that most Bitcoin transactions are legitimate, and the technology does not inherently facilitate criminal behavior.

Despite this, governments and regulatory authorities worldwide began to grapple with how to approach Bitcoin and other cryptocurrencies. Different countries adopted various regulatory approaches, ranging from outright bans to more accommodative frameworks. The regulatory landscape for cryptocurrencies continues to develop, reflecting the complexities of balancing innovation, consumer protection, and financial stability.

Bitcoin's early years were also marked by notable incidents, including hacking attacks on early exchanges and the emergence of alternative cryptocurrencies, commonly referred to as altcoins. These altcoins sought to address perceived shortcomings in Bitcoin's design and introduced novel features, such as increased transaction speed or enhanced privacy.

Perhaps one of the most significant developments during the early years of Bitcoin was the establishment of the Bitcoin Foundation in 2012. The foundation aimed to support the development and promotion of Bitcoin and its technology, advocating for its adoption and educating the public and policymakers about its potential benefits.

As Bitcoin gained more traction and attention, its price and market capitalization also experienced notable growth. In 2013, Bitcoin's price dramatically surged, attracting media attention and sparking public interest. This price rally was followed by increased scrutiny and volatility, as investors sought to capitalize on the digital currency's potential.

The year 2017 saw another unprecedented surge in Bitcoin's price, capturing global attention and drawing mainstream investors and speculators. The price reached new all-time highs, leading to discussions about a potential "Bitcoin bubble." The subsequent price correction sparked debates about cryptocurrencies' sustainability and long-term value.

As Bitcoin's popularity surged, so did its scalability challenges. The technology's limited transaction throughput and confirmation times led to congestion on the network during periods of high demand. This issue highlighted the need for solutions to enhance Bitcoin's capacity and improve transaction efficiency.

In response, the Bitcoin community explored various scaling solutions, including implementing Segregated Witness (SegWit) and the Lightning Network. SegWit, activated in 2017, allowed for more efficient use of block space, increasing the capacity for transactions. The Lightning Network, a second-layer solution built on top of Bitcoin's blockchain, aimed to enable faster and cheaper transactions by conducting them off-chain.

Despite the challenges and debates, Bitcoin's journey has been characterized by continuous development, innovation, and resilience. It has weathered various market cycles, regulatory changes, and technological challenges, evolving into a significant asset class and a store of value for investors seeking diversification and a hedge against traditional financial risks.

How Bitcoin mining works

Bitcoin mining lies at the heart of the cryptocurrency's decentralized design and ensures the security and integrity of its transactional ledger, the blockchain. This section explores the intricate process of Bitcoin mining, covering its role in confirming transactions, the concept of proof-of-work, mining hardware and software, mining pools, and the environmental impact of this energy-intensive process.

Bitcoin mining serves a crucial function in validating and confirming transactions on the blockchain. Whenever a user initiates a Bitcoin transaction, it is broadcasted to the network and enters a pool of unconfirmed transactions, known as the mempool. Miners select transactions from the mempool and include them in a candidate block, which they aim to add to the blockchain.

The core concept underpinning Bitcoin mining is proof-of-work (PoW). To add a new block to the blockchain, miners must solve a complex mathematical puzzle, known as the proof-of-work problem. This problem involves finding a specific number, called a nonce, that produces a hash with a certain number of leading zeros when combined with the block's data.

Finding the right nonce is akin to a trial-and-error method, as miners must make numerous attempts until they discover the correct solution. This process requires substantial computational power and electricity consumption, making Bitcoin mining a resource-intensive endeavor.

The first miner to find the correct nonce and produce a valid hash is rewarded with a block reward, which includes a fixed number of newly minted bitcoins and transaction fees collected from the included transactions. This process is called "finding a block," and the miner responsible for the successful block creation becomes the temporary central authority for validating and adding transactions to the blockchain.

Once a miner finds a block, they announce it to the network, and other miners verify its validity. This verification process confirms that the proof-of-work problem has been correctly solved and that the included transactions are valid and not double-spent. If most of the network's nodes agree on the block's validity, it is added to the blockchain, and the associated transactions are confirmed and considered irreversible.

The mining process is designed to be competitive and probabilistic. As more miners participate in the network, the competition to find the correct nonce and mine a block increases. The Bitcoin protocol adjusts the mining difficulty every 2,016 blocks (roughly every two weeks) to maintain an average block creation time of about 10 minutes. This adjustment helps ensure that new blocks are added to the blockchain relatively constantly.

Mining difficulty increases or decreases based on the network's collective computational power. When more miners participate in the network, the difficulty increases to maintain the 10-minute block time. Conversely, if miners leave the network, the difficulty decreases to incentivize more miners to participate.

As the Bitcoin network has expanded, mining has evolved from individual enthusiasts using CPUs and GPUs to specialized mining hardware called application-specific integrated circuits (ASICs). ASICs are custom-built chips designed exclusively for Bitcoin mining, offering significant efficiency and hash rate advantages.

Mining software plays a crucial role in the mining process. Miners use software to connect their mining hardware to the Bitcoin network and join mining pools. A mining pool is an organization of miners who merge their computational power in an effort to enhance their odds of finding a block and earning rewards.

In a mining pool, participants work together to solve the proof-of-work problem collectively. If any miner in the pool finds a valid block, the reward is distributed among the pool members according to their contributed hash rate. Pool mining allows individual miners with less powerful hardware to earn more consistent rewards over time, even if their likelihood of finding a block independently is relatively low.

The environmental influence of Bitcoin mining has been a concern, primarily due to the substantial energy consumption associated with the proof-of-work process. As mining difficulty increases and the number of miners grows, the energy requirements for mining also escalate.

Critics argue that Bitcoin mining's energy-intensive nature contributes to carbon emissions and environmental degradation. However, it is essential to contextualize Bitcoin's energy usage in the broader context of the global financial system. Traditional banking and financial systems consume significant amounts of energy for physical infrastructure, data centers, and everyday operations. In comparison, Bitcoin's energy consumption may represent a fraction of the overall energy used in the traditional financial system.

Furthermore, Bitcoin proponents argue that the cryptocurrency's decentralized and trustless nature justifies the energy expenditure. Bitcoin's security and immutability depend on the computational work required for mining, making it resistant to censorship and tampering.

Efforts are underway to explore alternative consensus mechanisms that do not rely on proof-of-work, such as proof-of-stake (PoS) and proof-of-authority (PoA). PoS relies on validators who are chosen to generate new blocks based on the amount of coins they store and are willing to "stake" as collateral. PoA relies on a set of known and trusted validators to verify transactions and create new blocks. These consensus mechanisms offer potential solutions to reduce energy consumption while maintaining the integrity and security of the blockchain.

Chapter IV
Decentralization and Blockchain Technology

Explaining blockchain technology

The revolutionary innovation known as blockchain technology has the power to upend entire sectors of the economy, change how businesses operate, and completely change how people interact with data and digital assets. This section delves into the fundamentals of blockchain technology, exploring its core concepts, decentralized architecture, cryptographic principles, use cases, and the challenges and opportunities it presents in various sectors.

Fundamentally, blockchain is a distributed as well as decentralized virtual ledger that keeps track of data and transactions among a node— a network of computers. Because every node in the network has a copy of the whole blockchain, redundancy and immutability are guaranteed. This design eliminates the need for a central authority or intermediary, as transactions are validated and agreed upon through a consensus mechanism among the network participants.

The cornerstone of blockchain's security and integrity lies in its cryptographic principles. A cryptographic hash, or unique digital fingerprint generated from the data contained in a block, is present in every block on the blockchain. This hash is also included in the subsequent block, linking all blocks together chronologically. Any tampering with the data in a block would result in a change in its hash, which the other nodes in the network would immediately detect.

Blockchain's consensus mechanism is the process by which nodes concur on the validity of transactions and add them to the blockchain. Various consensus mechanisms are designed to suit different use cases and network requirements. The most well-known consensus mechanism is proof-of-work (PoW), used by Bitcoin and many other cryptocurrencies. In PoW, miners compete to solve complicated mathematical puzzles, with the first one to find the correct solution being able to add a new block to the blockchain. This competitive process ensures that no single entity can control the network, making it resilient to attacks and censorship.

Another popular consensus mechanism is proof-of-stake (PoS), used by cryptocurrencies such as Ethereum. In PoS, validators are selected to create new blocks depending on the amount of coins they have and are willing to "stake" as collateral. PoS consumes significantly reduced energy than PoW and offers potential scalability benefits, but it has its unique challenges, such as the "nothing at stake" problem.

A key element of blockchain technology are smart contracts, which enable the programmable contracts to execute on their own when certain circumstances are satisfied. Smart contracts enable automated and transparent interactions without intermediaries, enhancing the efficiency and trustworthiness of various processes across industries.

Blockchain technology has found numerous applications across diverse sectors. In finance, blockchain has disrupted traditional systems by enabling fast and low-cost cross-border payments through cryptocurrencies, bypassing the need for intermediaries like banks. Additionally, blockchain's transparent and auditable nature has facilitated the tokenization of assets, such as real estate and artworks, opening up new opportunities for fractional ownership and liquidity.

Supply chain management is another different area where blockchain has shown significant potential. Blockchain enhances transparency and traceability by creating an immutable record of the entire supply chain process, from production to distribution. This can help combat counterfeit products, improve quality control, and ensure ethical sourcing of goods.

Blockchain's impact is not limited to financial and industrial sectors. It has also revolutionized the digital art world through the rise of non-fungible tokens (NFTs). NFTs are unique digital assets representing ownership of digital art, music, collectibles, and more. These tokens are recorded on the blockchain, ensuring the digital assets' provenance and scarcity, enabling artists to monetize their creations in new ways.

Moreover, blockchain technology has implications for identity management and privacy. Self-sovereign identity systems based on blockchain empower individuals to control their digital identities and personal data, reducing the risks of data breaches and identity theft. Blockchain's encryption and permissioning mechanisms also enable secure data sharing between parties while preserving privacy.

Despite its promise, blockchain technology faces several challenges. Scalability remains a key concern, particularly for public blockchains with high transaction volumes. As the number of transactions increases, block sizes and validation times can become bottlenecks. Various solutions, such as layer 2 protocols like the Lightning Network for Bitcoin and sharding for Ethereum, are being explored to address these scalability issues.

Interoperability between different blockchain networks is another challenge that hinders the seamless exchange of assets and data across platforms. Efforts are underway to develop cross-chain bridges and standards to enable interoperability and enhance the overall blockchain ecosystem's efficiency.

Moreover, blockchain's environmental impact has drawn criticism due to the energy-intensive nature of proof-of-work consensus mechanisms. As the acceptance for cryptocurrencies and blockchain applications grows, exploring more energy-efficient consensus mechanisms, such as proof-of-stake, and implementing sustainable mining practices is necessary.

Regulatory and legal challenges also surround blockchain technology. Governments and regulatory bodies are still grappling on how to address cryptocurrencies, ICOs (Initial Coin Offerings), and smart contracts within existing legal frameworks. Balancing innovation and consumer protection while addressing potential risks and fraudulent activities remains complex.

Despite these challenges, the ability of blockchain technology continues to inspire innovation and investment in diverse fields. Governments, businesses, and researchers worldwide are exploring blockchain's transformative potential and investing in its development. As blockchain technology evolves and matures, its impact will likely extend far beyond its current applications, shaping the future of finance, commerce, governance, and societal interactions.

Advantages of decentralization

Decentralization, a fundamental principle of various systems and technologies, offers many advantages across economic, political, social, and technological spheres. In this section, we explore the numerous benefits of decentralization, including increased resilience, enhanced security, improved transparency, greater inclusivity, and its potential to foster innovation and empower individuals in the digital age.

One of the primary advantages of decentralization is its inherent resilience and robustness in the face of failures and attacks. Traditional centralized systems are vulnerable to single points of failure, where the malfunctioning of a central authority can disrupt the entire system. In contrast, decentralized systems distribute authority and control across a network of nodes, reducing the impact of individual node failures. This redundancy makes decentralized networks more resistant to outages, ensuring continuity and reliability of services even in challenging conditions.

Decentralization also enhances security by minimizing the risk of data breaches and hacking attacks. In centralized systems, a breach of the central server can compromise sensitive information, leading to severe consequences for individuals and organizations. Decentralized technologies like blockchain utilize cryptographic principles and consensus mechanisms to secure data and ensure its integrity. By keeping data across a distributed network, blockchain prevents unauthorized modifications and tampering, creating a tamper-proof and transparent record of transactions and events.

Moreover, decentralization promotes transparency and accountability. In centralized systems, decision-making and data management often occur behind closed doors, limiting public scrutiny and oversight. On the other hand, decentralized systems enable transparent governance, where actions and changes are publicly recorded and accessible to all network participants. This transparency fosters trust and allows stakeholders to hold decision-makers accountable for their actions, ensuring fairness and reducing the potential for corruption and abuse of power.

Decentralization is also closely associated with the principle of inclusivity. Centralized systems can be exclusionary, favoring privileged individuals or groups while marginalizing others.

Decentralized networks, especially in the context of cryptocurrencies and blockchain technology, provide greater financial inclusion by granting access to financial services to those who lack traditional banking facilities. Additionally, decentralized platforms enable permissionless participation, allowing anyone with an internet connection to join and contribute to the network.

Furthermore, decentralization has the potential to foster innovation and creativity. Traditional centralized systems often impose stringent rules and requirements, making it challenging for new ideas and technologies to flourish. In contrast, decentralized networks provide fertile ground for experimentation, enabling developers to create and deploy novel applications and services without gatekeepers or intermediaries. This open and permissionless environment encourages rapid iteration and collaboration, fueling innovation and discovering new solutions to existing problems.

Decentralization is particularly empowering for individuals in the digital age. Centralized platforms, such as social media and e-commerce giants, often collect vast amounts of user data, which can be monetized or used without individuals' consent. In decentralized systems, users have more control over their data and digital identities, allowing them to choose how and when their information is shared. Based on decentralized principles, self-sovereign identity systems empower individuals to manage and protect their digital identities, mitigating the risk of identity theft and data breaches.

The advantages of decentralization also extend to governance and decision-making processes. Decentralized governance models, often seen in decentralized autonomous organizations (DAOs), allow stakeholders to participate directly in decision-making through voting and consensus mechanisms. This bottom-up approach ensures that decisions reflect the community's will and are not dictated solely by a central authority or small group of individuals.

Decentralization also has the potential to promote economic empowerment and reduce income inequality. In centralized financial systems, access to capital and financial services may be limited to certain privileged groups, excluding many individuals from participating in the economy. Decentralized finance (DeFi) platforms, enabled by blockchain technology, offer opportunities for peer-to-peer lending, borrowing, and investing, democratizing access to financial instruments and leveling the playing field for participants.

Furthermore, decentralization can have positive environmental implications. Traditional centralized data centers consume vast amounts of energy for cooling and maintenance, contributing to carbon emissions and environmental degradation. Decentralized systems, especially those based on proof-of-stake consensus mechanisms, consume significantly less energy, making them more environmentally friendly and sustainable.

Despite the many advantages, decentralization is not without its challenges. Scaling decentralized systems to accommodate increasing demand remains a significant obstacle. As more users join decentralized networks, the computational and storage requirements can strain the network's capacity. Solutions like layer 2 protocols and sharding are being explored to address scalability challenges.

Interoperability between different decentralized networks is another issue that hinders the seamless exchange of assets and data. Efforts are underway to develop cross-chain solutions and standards to enable better interoperability and enhance the overall efficiency of the decentralized ecosystem.

Moreover, the lack of centralized governance can make decision-making more complex and contentious in decentralized networks. Achieving consensus among stakeholders with diverse interests and incentives may require innovative governance models and mechanisms to maintain a cohesive and functioning ecosystem.

Key features of the Bitcoin blockchain

As the foundational technology behind the world's first decentralized cryptocurrency, the Bitcoin blockchain possesses several key features that have revolutionized the financial landscape. This section explores the fundamental characteristics of the Bitcoin blockchain, including its decentralized nature, transparency and immutability, proof-of-work consensus mechanism, limited supply, and pseudonymous transactions. These features collectively contribute to Bitcoin's resilience, security, and widespread adoption, making it a unique and transformative digital asset.

At the core of the Bitcoin blockchain lies its decentralized nature. Unlike traditional financial systems, which rely on central authorities to manage and validate transactions, the Bitcoin blockchain operates on a peer-to-peer network of nodes. Each node holds a copy of the full blockchain, ensuring redundancy and eliminating single points of failure. This decentralized architecture means no single entity or organization controls the network, making it censorship-resistant and resilient to attacks.

Another essential feature of the Bitcoin blockchain is its transparency and immutability. Every transaction on the blockchain are publicly recorded in blocks, and each block is linked to the previous one through cryptographic hashes. Once a block is added to the blockchain, its data becomes immutable and cannot be altered or erased. This permanence ensures the integrity of transaction records and prevents fraud and double-spending, providing a transparent and tamper-proof ledger for financial transactions.

The proof-of-work (PoW) consensus mechanism is critical to the Bitcoin blockchain's security. In PoW, miners compete to solve complicated mathematical puzzles, with the first one to find the correct solution earning the right to add a new block to the blockchain. This process requires significant computational power, making it computationally infeasible for malicious actors to manipulate the blockchain. PoW ensures that most network participants agree on the validity of transactions, making the network more secure and resistant to attacks.

The Bitcoin blockchain's limited supply is another defining feature that differentiates it from traditional fiat currencies. As specified in the Bitcoin protocol, the total bitcoin supply is capped at 21 million. This scarcity is achieved through a predetermined issuance rate that halves approximately every four years, an event known as the "halving." The limited supply of bitcoins serves as a hedge against inflation and has contributed to its perception as digital gold and a store of value.

Furthermore, the Bitcoin blockchain ensures pseudonymous transactions, providing a degree of privacy to users. The wallet addresses of the people involved are not directly connected to their identities, even though the transactions are publicly documented on the blockchain. Instead, users are identified by alphanumeric strings, allowing for a degree of privacy in their financial activities. However, it is essential to recognize that Bitcoin transactions are not entirely anonymous, as blockchain analysis techniques can potentially trace the flow of funds and reveal transaction patterns.

Combining these key features makes the Bitcoin blockchain a transformative technology that has reshaped the financial landscape. Its decentralized nature eliminates the need for intermediaries, reducing transaction costs and improving financial inclusion. The transparency and immutability of the blockchain provide a trustless and auditable record of transactions, promoting accountability and reducing the risk of fraud.

Moreover, the security offered by the PoW consensus mechanism makes the Bitcoin blockchain resilient to attacks and censorship, ensuring the integrity of the network even in challenging conditions. The limited supply of bitcoins fosters a perception of scarcity, driving demand and contributing to its value as a digital asset and a potential hedge against economic uncertainty.

Despite its many advantages, the Bitcoin blockchain also faces challenges and limitations. The PoW consensus mechanism's energy-intensive nature has raised concerns about its environmental impact, prompting discussions about alternative consensus mechanisms like proof-of-stake, which consume significantly less energy.

Additionally, the scalability of the Bitcoin blockchain has been a topic of debate. As the number of transactions increases, block sizes and validation times can become bottlenecks, leading to congestion on the network. Efforts are underway to explore solutions, such as implementing second-layer protocols like the Lightning Network, to address scalability issues.

Furthermore, the pseudonymous nature of Bitcoin transactions has drawn attention from regulators and policymakers, as it can be used for illicit activities. Balancing privacy and compliance remain a challenge for the cryptocurrency industry.

Chapter V
How Bitcoin Transactions Work

Public and private keys

Public and private keys are essential to modern cryptographic systems, providing the foundation for secure communication, digital signatures, and authentication. This section explores the concept of public and private keys, how they work together in asymmetric encryption algorithms, their applications in various fields, and the importance of safeguarding these keys to ensure the integrity and confidentiality of sensitive information.

At the heart of asymmetric encryption lies the concept of public and private keys. In this cryptographic system, each user is assigned a unique key pair consisting of public and private keys. These keys are mathematically related, but while the public key can be openly shared with everyone, the private key must be kept confidential and known only to the owner.

The public key is the user's address in the cryptographic world. It is used to encrypt data or messages intended for the user. Anyone can utilize the public key to encrypt information, but only the owner of the corresponding private key can decrypt and access the original data. This property forms the basis of secure communication and confidentiality.

Conversely, the private key is used for decryption. It is kept secret by the owner and should never be shared or exposed to others. When users receive encrypted data intended for them, they use their private key to decrypt and access the original information. The private key is the critical piece that ensures the confidentiality of sensitive data and prevents unauthorized access.

The RSA (Rivest–Shamir–Adleman) algorithm is one of the most well-known asymmetric encryption algorithms. In RSA, the system's security relies on the difficulty of factoring sizable composite numbers into their prime factors. The public key in RSA consists of two parts: the modulus (a product of two large prime numbers) and the public exponent. The private key contains the same modulus and a different private exponent. Together, these components enable secure encryption and decryption processes.

Asymmetric encryption has numerous applications across various fields, especially in the realm of secure communication and data integrity. Secure Socket Layer (or SSL) and Transport Layer Security (or TLS) protocols, used to encrypt data during online communication, rely on public and private keys to establish secure connections between clients and servers. This guarantees that sensitive information, such as credit card details and passwords, remains encrypted and protected during transmission.

Digital signatures are another important application of public and private keys. In digital signatures, the sender uses their private key to generate a special digital signature for a message or document. The recipient can then verify the signature using the sender's public key to ensure the message's authenticity and integrity. Digital signatures are widely used in electronic documents, contracts, and authentication processes, providing a way to verify the legitimacy of digital content.

The field of cryptocurrencies also heavily relies on public and private keys for security and user authentication. Each user in a cryptocurrency network has a unique key pair that allows them to send and receive digital assets securely. The public key serves as the wallet address, and the private key grants access to the funds. Safeguarding the private key is of utmost importance in cryptocurrencies, as it is the only way to access and control the assets associated with a certain wallet address.

Public and private keys have also found applications in identity management and access control. Public key infrastructure (PKI) systems use digital certificates to bind public keys to individuals or entities, creating a trust network for secure communications. These certificates, issued by certificate authorities (CAs), provide a way to verify the authenticity of a public key and the identity of its owner.

Despite their inherent security advantages, public and private keys have challenges. Key management is a critical aspect of cryptographic systems, as the compromise of a private key can lead to catastrophic consequences, like data breaches and identity theft.

Various strategies, such as hardware security modules (HSMs) and multi-factor authentication, are employed to enhance the security of private keys and mitigate the risks associated with key exposure.

Another challenge lies in key distribution. In asymmetric encryption, users must securely obtain each other's public keys to establish secure communication. This process can be vulnerable to man-in-the-middle attacks, where an attacker intercepts communication and presents their own public key to both parties. Solutions such as digital certificates and trusted third parties help address this challenge and ensure the authenticity of public keys.

Moreover, the computational complexity of asymmetric encryption algorithms can be a drawback for resource-constrained environments. Encrypting and decrypting data using private and public keys can be computationally demanding, especially for large datasets. To reach a balance between performance and security, hybrid encryption systems—which combine the security of asymmetric encryption with the efficiency of symmetric encryption—are therefore frequently used.

Wallets and addresses

Wallets and addresses are integral components of the cryptocurrency ecosystem, providing users with the means to store, send, and receive digital assets securely. This section explores the concept of cryptocurrency wallets and addresses, the different types of wallets available, their underlying technologies, security considerations, and their role in facilitating seamless and trustless transactions in the decentralized financial landscape.

Cryptocurrency wallets serve as digital containers that store cryptographic keys used to access and manage users' digital assets, like bitcoins and other cryptocurrencies. These wallets are not physical objects but software applications or hardware devices that interact with the blockchain to let users to send and receive cryptocurrencies securely.

Cryptocurrency wallets are broadly categorized into two main types: hot and cold wallets. Because of their internet connectivity, hot wallets are more vulnerable to cyberattacks. They are convenient for frequent transactions and easy access but may present higher security risks. On the other hand, cold wallets are not connected to the internet and are considered more secure. They are often used for long-term storage of cryptocurrencies, reducing the risk of unauthorized access.

Hot wallets include web wallets, mobile wallets, and desktop wallets. Web wallets are hosted by third-party service providers and accessible through web browsers, making them convenient for users accessing their cryptocurrencies from different devices. As the name suggests, mobile wallets are designed for mobile devices and offer portability and ease of use. Desktop wallets are software applications installed on personal computers, giving users more control over their private keys.

Cold wallets encompass hardware wallets and paper wallets. Hardware wallets are tangible devices specifically designed to store private keys offline, providing an extra layer of security. These devices generate and sign offline transactions, keeping the private keys from potential online threats. On the other hand, paper wallets involve printing the private key and public address on a physical piece of paper. While paper wallets offer an air-gapped solution, users must take extra precautions to protect the physical copies from damage and unauthorized access.

Cryptocurrency addresses are alphanumeric strings that serve as unique identifiers for cryptocurrency transactions. They are derived from the user's public key and are used to send and receive cryptocurrencies. For example, in Bitcoin, addresses are generated based on the elliptic curve cryptography (ECC) algorithm and are encoded using Base58Check encoding. Ethereum addresses, on the other hand, are generated based on the secp256k1 elliptic curve and are encoded using Base58 encoding.

Cryptocurrency addresses are crucial for facilitating transactions on the blockchain. Users who want to receive cryptocurrency share their public address with the sender. The sender uses the recipient's public address to create a transaction and transfer the specified amount of cryptocurrency. The transaction is then validated by miners and added to the blockchain, updating the respective wallet's balance.

It is important to note that cryptocurrency addresses are case-sensitive and must be entered accurately to ensure successful transactions. Sending funds to a wrong address may result in permanent loss of the assets, as blockchain transactions are irreversible.

Cryptocurrency addresses are also essential for verifying the authenticity of transactions. For instance, in the context of Bitcoin, anyone can verify the ownership of a Bitcoin address by checking the blockchain and confirming that the corresponding public key is associated with the address. This public nature of the blockchain provides transparency and accountability, as all transactions are publicly recorded and auditable.

The security of cryptocurrency wallets and addresses is paramount, given the irreversible nature of blockchain transactions. One of the primary security considerations is the management of private keys. In a custodial wallet service, where a third-party holds the users' private keys on their behalf, users must trust the provider to secure their funds adequately. On the other hand, non-custodial wallets, give users complete control over their private keys, giving them the responsibility for ensuring the security of their assets.

Hardware wallets offer high security by keeping private keys offline and isolated from potential online threats. The use of hardware wallets can protect against malware, phishing attacks, and other forms of cyberattacks. In order to prevent any vulnerabilities, it is imperative that hardware wallets be purchased from reliable suppliers and that best practices be followed when configuring and utilizing these devices.

Another security feature that shields cryptocurrency wallets is multi-factor authentication (MFA). Before being able to use their wallet, users using MFA must submit various kinds of identity, which include a password and a one-time verification code texted to their mobile device. This lowers the possibility of unwanted access even in the event that a password is stolen.

For software wallets, keeping the operating system and wallet software up to date with the most current security patches is vital to mitigate potential vulnerabilities. Users should also enable encryption on their devices and practice good password management to prevent unauthorized access.

In the case of paper wallets, the physical copies must be stored in a secure and controlled environment, away from prying eyes and potential hazards like fire or water damage. Users should also consider creating multiple copies of paper wallets and storing them in separate secure locations to avoid complete loss in case one copy is damaged or lost.

Phishing attacks and scams are common in cryptocurrency, targeting users to trick them into revealing their private keys or credentials. Users should exercise caution and verify the authenticity of any requests for their private keys or passwords, especially when dealing with unsolicited communication or suspicious websites.

Transaction verification and confirmation

Transaction verification and confirmation are fundamental processes in the Bitcoin network, ensuring the integrity and security of the decentralized financial system. This section explores how transactions are verified, the role of miners in the confirmation process, the concept of block propagation, the significance of the block size limit, and the factors that affect transaction speed and fees in the Bitcoin network.

When a user starts a Bitcoin transaction, it is announce to the network and added to the transaction pool, also known as the memory pool or mempool. The transaction pool contains all unconfirmed transactions waiting to be included in a new block. For a transaction to be valid, it must adhere to the rules and protocols of the Bitcoin network, such as not spending more bitcoins than are available in the sender's address and including the required transaction fee.

Transaction verification in Bitcoin relies on a consensus mechanism known as proof-of-work (PoW). Miners, who are participants in the network with computational power, compete to solve a complex mathematical puzzle known as the "hash puzzle" or "proof-of-work problem." The first miner to find the correct solution is granted the right to create a new block and include a set of valid transactions in it.

The process of solving the proof-of-work problem is computationally intensive and requires significant computational power. The network adjusts the puzzle's difficulty approximately every two weeks to maintain an average block creation time of around 10 minutes. As more miners participate in the network, the competition to find the solution increases, ensuring a secure and decentralized network.

Once a miner successfully solves the proof-of-work problem, they create a new block containing the selected transactions from the mempool. This block also includes a special transaction known as the coinbase transaction, which rewards the miner with newly minted bitcoins and any transaction fees collected from the included transactions. The coinbase transaction is the only type of transaction that does not require inputs and can create new bitcoins out of thin air.

After a miner creates a new block, they broadcast it to the network, and other nodes in the network validate the block and its contents. The validation process includes checking the correctness of each transaction, verifying that the block satisfies the proof-of-work requirements, and ensuring that the block does not conflict with any other previously validated blocks. If the block is valid, other nodes in the network will add it to their copy of the blockchain.

The transactions included in a block are regarded as confirmed once it is added to the blockchain. The quantity of blocks that have been added to the blockchain subsequent to the block that contains the transaction indicates the number of confirmations associated with that transaction. For example, if a transaction is included in the block at height 100, and the current block height is 110, the transaction is said to have ten confirmations.

The concept of confirmations is essential for the security and finality of transactions in the Bitcoin network. As more blocks are added to the blockchain after the block containing the transaction, reversing or altering the transaction becomes increasingly difficult.

For transactions with multiple confirmations, the likelihood of a double-spending attack, where an attacker tries to spend the same bitcoins twice, becomes negligible.

The block propagation process is a critical aspect of transaction confirmation in Bitcoin. As miners create new blocks, they must broadcast them to other network nodes. The time it takes for a block to propagate across the network can affect the confirmation time of transactions. A fast and efficient block propagation mechanism is essential to maintain a low confirmation time and avoid potential forks or temporary divergences in the blockchain.

One challenge in block propagation is the block size limit, a parameter introduced in the Bitcoin protocol to prevent blocks from becoming too large. Initially set to 1 MB, the block size limit was designed to protect the network from potential denial-of-service attacks by limiting the amount of data that can be included in a single block. However, as the popularity of Bitcoin grew, the block size limit became a source of debate and controversy.

As the number of transactions in the Bitcoin network increased, the limited block size led to congestion and higher transaction fees during peak periods. To address this issue, several proposals were introduced, including increasing the block size limit through a hard fork. However, achieving consensus on such changes proved challenging, leading to the generation of Bitcoin Cash, a cryptocurrency that increased the block size limit to 8 MB.

To address the issue of scalability, the Bitcoin community explored various solutions, such as Segregated Witness (SegWit) and the Lightning Network. SegWit was activated in August 2017 and introduced a new transaction format that separated the transaction signature data (witness) from the transaction data, effectively increasing the effective block size. The Lightning Network serves as a layer-2 scaling solution that enables faster and lower-cost transactions by creating off-chain payment channels.

The transaction speed and fees in the Bitcoin network are influenced by various factors, including the number of transactions in the mempool, the level of network congestion, and the transaction fee selected by the sender. Users may pay a higher transaction fee to encourage miners to prioritize their transactions in instances where the network is highly congested and there are a lot of pending transactions.

Bitcoin wallets and various cryptocurrency services often allow users to choose the transaction fee based on their desired confirmation time. While transactions with lower costs could take longer to confirm, those with higher fees are more probable to be included in the following block. Miners are still able to choose which transactions to include in their blocks, therefore the size of the transaction fee does not ensure instant confirmation.

Ensuring effective and safe mechanisms for transaction verification and confirmation is crucial to maintaining the integrity and dependability of the decentralized financial ecosystem as Bitcoin as well as other cryptocurrencies continue to gain popularity. Ongoing research and development in the field of blockchain technology will undoubtedly contribute to improving the scalability and performance of cryptocurrency networks, further enhancing the user experience and adoption of digital currencies.

Chapter VI
Bitcoin's Rise to Prominence

Early adoption and use cases

Bitcoin, the world's first decentralized cryptocurrency, was introduced in 2009 by Satoshi Nakamoto, an anonymous individual or group. In its early days, Bitcoin garnered attention from a niche group of enthusiasts and technologists who recognized its disruptive potential. This section explores the early adoption and use cases of Bitcoin, from its humble beginnings as an experimental digital currency to its transformation into a global phenomenon with diverse applications in finance, remittances, e-commerce, and more.

In its early years, Bitcoin adoption was limited to a relatively small community of tech-savvy individuals who were drawn to its innovative properties. One of the primary motivations for early adopters was the concept of decentralization, which removed the need for intermediaries like banks and governments to conduct financial transactions. Early supporters of Bitcoin saw it as a way to challenge the traditional financial system and promote financial freedom and autonomy.

The emergence of online marketplaces and forums, such as the Silk Road, also played a role in early Bitcoin adoption. The Silk Road, an underground marketplace operating on the dark web, enabled users to buy and sell goods and services using Bitcoin as a means of payment. Although authorities eventually shut down the Silk Road due to its association with illicit activities, it contributed to the early adoption of Bitcoin as a medium of exchange for both legal and illegal transactions.

As Bitcoin gained traction within the tech community, its utility as a peer-to-peer electronic cash system became more evident. Users found that Bitcoin could be used to send and receive funds globally, with lower fees and faster transaction times than traditional banking systems. Additionally, Bitcoin transactions offered privacy and pseudonymity that appealed to users seeking more control over their financial information.

Remittances, particularly for individuals in countries with limited access to traditional banking services, were among the earliest practical use cases of Bitcoin. Bitcoin's borderless and frictionless nature allowed migrants to send money back home to their families at lower costs than traditional remittance services. This use case provided an essential lifeline for many individuals in regions with high remittance costs and limited financial infrastructure.

Another significant early use case for Bitcoin was its online crowdfunding and fundraising role. Bitcoin made it easier for individuals and organizations to accept donations and contributions from a global audience without the need for traditional banking channels. This was particularly beneficial for non-profit organizations and projects that faced challenges in receiving funding due to geographical or regulatory restrictions.

The decentralized nature of Bitcoin also made it an attractive choice for businesses and individuals seeking to bypass capital controls and restrictions in certain countries. Bitcoin allowed individuals to preserve and move their wealth outside of traditional banking systems in regions with unstable economies and strict capital outflow regulations.

Over time, Bitcoin's growing acceptance and integration into various industries led to an expansion of its use cases. Online merchants and businesses started accepting Bitcoin as a form of payment, allowing customers to purchase goods and services with the digital currency. Major companies such as Microsoft, Expedia, and Overstock were among the early adopters to embrace Bitcoin payments.

In addition to e-commerce, the gaming industry also saw the potential of Bitcoin as a payment method. Online gaming platforms and virtual marketplaces began accepting Bitcoin for in-game purchases and microtransactions. Integrating Bitcoin into gaming ecosystems opened up new opportunities for cross-border transactions and increased accessibility for gamers worldwide.

Furthermore, Bitcoin's utility as a hedge against inflation and economic uncertainty attracted investors seeking to diversify their portfolios. As a non-correlated asset, Bitcoin protected wealth in times of economic instability and served as a potential store of value alongside traditional assets like gold.

The potential for using Bitcoin as a means of cross-border remittances and international trade also received attention from financial institutions and governments. The speed and lower transaction fees offered by Bitcoin compared to traditional banking systems made it an appealing option for international money transfers. Some governments and central banks even explored the concept of issuing their digital currencies, often called Central Bank Digital Currencies (CBDCs), in response to the rise of cryptocurrencies like Bitcoin.

As Bitcoin gained mainstream attention, its price experienced significant fluctuations and speculative interest. While attracting investors seeking profit opportunities, this volatility also raised concerns about its suitability as a stable currency for everyday transactions. Critics argued that Bitcoin's price volatility and lack of regulatory oversight could hinder its mass adoption as a mainstream currency.

Despite these challenges, Bitcoin's early adoption laid the groundwork for developing the broader cryptocurrency ecosystem. As the first cryptocurrency, Bitcoin paved the way for creating thousands of alternative cryptocurrencies, known as altcoins, each with unique features and applications. The early enthusiasm and experimentation with Bitcoin catalyzed innovation in blockchain technology and decentralized applications.

Media attention and controversies

Bitcoin has been the focus of several debates and received a lot of media attention since its launch in 2009. As the world's first decentralized cryptocurrency, Bitcoin's rise to prominence has sparked both fascination and skepticism among journalists, economists, and policymakers. This section explores the media attention that Bitcoin has received over the years, the controversies surrounding its use in illicit activities, its environmental impact, and the ongoing debates about its potential as a disruptive technology and a viable alternative to traditional financial systems.

Bitcoin first gained media attention in its early years through tech-centric publications and online forums. The mysterious identity of its creator, Satoshi Nakamoto, and the concept of a peer-to-peer digital currency fascinated readers and attracted the interest of early adopters. As Bitcoin's value started to increase, mainstream media outlets began covering the cryptocurrency more extensively, leading to a surge in public awareness.

The meteoric rise of Bitcoin's price in 2017 brought the cryptocurrency to the forefront of global media attention. News outlets across the globe were dominated by headlines about Bitcoin's phenomenal price increases, which reached an all-time high of approximately $20,000 in December 2017. This "crypto mania" period led to a wave of interest from retail investors and speculators, further amplifying media coverage.

As Bitcoin gained popularity, it also became associated with controversies and illicit activities. One of the earliest and most infamous use cases of Bitcoin was its association with the Silk Road, an underground marketplace on the dark web. The Silk Road facilitated the buying and selling of illegal drugs and other illicit goods using Bitcoin as a means of payment. The shutdown of the Silk Road by authorities in 2013 brought Bitcoin's use in illegal activities to the forefront of media attention.

Bitcoin's pseudonymous nature, allowing users to transact without revealing their real-world identities, raised concerns about its potential for money laundering, tax evasion, and other financial crimes. Critics argued that the lack of transparency in Bitcoin transactions made it attractive to criminals seeking to evade law enforcement.

Media reports of high-profile hacks and thefts from cryptocurrency exchanges also contributed to Bitcoin's association with criminal activities. Several exchanges, including Mt. Gox and Bitfinex, experienced large-scale security breaches, causing the loss of Bitcoin and other cryptocurrencies valued at millions of dollars. These incidents fueled skepticism about the security and reliability of digital assets.

Another controversial aspect of Bitcoin is its environmental impact, particularly its energy consumption. Bitcoin's consensus mechanism, proof-of-work (PoW), requires miners to compete to solve complex mathematical puzzles requiring significant computational power and energy.

As the Bitcoin network has grown, so has its energy consumption. Critics argue that the environmental cost of Bitcoin mining, particularly in regions where electricity generation relies heavily on fossil fuels, contradicts the global efforts to combat climate change. Media outlets have reported on the ecological footprint of Bitcoin mining, leading to debates about the sustainability of the cryptocurrency.

Bitcoin's decentralized and borderless nature has presented regulatory and legal challenges for governments worldwide. Policymakers have grappled with classifying and regulating cryptocurrencies within existing financial frameworks.

Media attention often focuses on government responses to Bitcoin, ranging from outright bans in some countries to more permissive regulations in others. The lack of uniformity in regulatory approaches has created uncertainty for businesses and investors operating in the cryptocurrency space.

Bitcoin's price volatility has been a recurrent topic of media coverage. With the cryptocurrency experiencing both rapid gains and steep declines, dramatic price fluctuations have attracted investors seeking to profit from its price movements.

Media outlets have often highlighted the speculative nature of Bitcoin, warning readers about the risks associated with investing in a highly volatile asset. The fear of missing out (FOMO) during price rallies and the fear of missing out (FUD) during downturns have been recurring themes in media coverage.

Amid controversies and skepticism, Bitcoin has also been covered as a potential disruptive technology that can revolutionize the financial landscape. Media reports have explored how blockchain technology, the underlying technology of Bitcoin, could transform various industries beyond finance, like supply chain management, healthcare, and voting systems.

Bitcoin's potential as a hedge against inflation and economic instability has also been a subject of media attention, particularly during times of economic uncertainty. Reports have analyzed how individuals and institutional investors view Bitcoin as a store of value that is similar to digital gold.

Media outlets have hosted debates and discussions about the long-term viability of Bitcoin and its potential to coexist with or replace traditional financial systems. Some economists and finance experts view Bitcoin as a speculative bubble destined to burst, while others consider it a legitimate financial asset with the potential for significant growth.

The scalability and usability of Bitcoin as a global payment system have also been topics of media coverage. Critics point to the limited transaction throughput and long confirmation times during network congestion as hurdles to mainstream adoption. On the other hand, proponents highlight ongoing research and development efforts, such as implementing the Lightning Network and other layer-2 solutions, as potential solutions to scalability challenges.

Media attention, controversies, and debates have marked Bitcoin's journey from obscurity to global fame. As the first cryptocurrency, Bitcoin has captured the imagination of millions and triggered discussions about the future of money, finance, and technology.

Media coverage has been crucial in shaping public perceptions of Bitcoin, from portraying it as a revolutionary technology with the ability to disrupt traditional finance to associating it with illicit activities and speculative excesses. While the controversies and challenges Bitcoin faces have been significant, they have also driven innovation and awareness of the broader blockchain ecosystem.

As cryptocurrency evolves, media attention will remain a key influencer of public sentiment and regulatory approaches. Reporting on the developments, challenges, and innovations in the cryptocurrency world will contribute to a better understanding of Bitcoin's place in the global financial landscape and its potential to shape the future of decentralized technologies.

Bitcoin's price fluctuations and market cycles

Bitcoin's price fluctuations and market cycles have been a defining characteristic of the cryptocurrency's journey since its inception in 2009. This section explores the factors contributing to Bitcoin's price volatility, the patterns observed in its market cycles, the role of supply and demand dynamics, and the significance of understanding market cycles for investors and stakeholders in the cryptocurrency ecosystem.

Bitcoin's price volatility is one of the most distinctive features of the cryptocurrency. Unlike traditional assets like stocks or fiat currencies, which typically experience relatively stable price movements, Bitcoin's value can fluctuate significantly over short periods. These fluctuations can lead to rapid price appreciation and equally swift declines, making Bitcoin an asset that attracts risk-seeking investors and cautious skeptics.

Several factors contribute to Bitcoin's price volatility. Firstly, the relatively small market size of cryptocurrencies, compared to traditional financial markets, means that large buy or sell orders can disproportionately impact prices. As a result, even seemingly minor events or news can lead to significant price swings.

Secondly, the absence of a central authority regulating Bitcoin's price contributes to its volatility. Unlike fiat currencies, which central banks and governments manage, Bitcoin's value is primarily determined by market sentiment, demand, and supply. This decentralized nature means that no single entity can control or stabilize the price of Bitcoin.

Moreover, the cryptocurrency space's relatively nascent and speculative nature plays a role in price volatility. As a new asset class, cryptocurrencies are subject to investor sentiment, news-driven speculation, and rapidly evolving technological developments, all of which can trigger price movements.

Bitcoin's price history has exhibited a series of market cycles, characterized by periods of rapid price appreciation followed by sharp corrections. These cycles are often referred to as "boom and bust" cycles and have been observed multiple times in Bitcoin's existence.

The boom phase of the market cycle is marked by a surge in demand and speculative fervor, driving prices to new all-time highs. During these periods, media attention and public interest in Bitcoin typically reach a peak, with a surge in retail and institutional investment. Narratives of Bitcoin often accompany the euphoria of the boom phase as a "digital gold" and a hedge against inflation and economic instability.

However, the boom phase is often followed by a sharp correction, where prices experience a significant decline from their peak levels. Factors such as profit-taking by early investors, market sentiment shifts, and regulatory developments can trigger these corrections. The correction phase can also be exacerbated by margin trading and leverage, where traders borrow funds to magnify their positions, leading to higher volatility.

Following the correction phase, the market typically enters a consolidation period characterized by relatively stable prices and reduced volatility. During this phase, the market participants assess the developments and fundamentals of the cryptocurrency, and a new wave of adoption and innovation begins to build.

The cycle then repeats itself, with periods of accumulation and slow price appreciation, leading to another boom phase, correction, and consolidation. While the timing and magnitude of each cycle can vary, the boom and bust nature of Bitcoin's market cycles has remained a recurring pattern over the years.

Bitcoin's fixed supply is another critical factor in its price fluctuations and market cycles. Bitcoin has a restricted supply of 21 million coins, in contrast to fiat currencies, which central banks can produce as many as they desire. This scarcity means increased demand for Bitcoin, whether driven by speculative interest or genuine utility, can lead to price appreciation.

The halving events occur approximately every four years and play a significant role in Bitcoin's supply and demand dynamics. During a halving event, the block reward for miners is cut in half, reducing the rate at which new bitcoins are created. This halving cycle effectively decreases the new bitcoin supply entering the market, potentially leading to a supply shock.

Historically, halving events have been followed by periods of significant price appreciation, as the reduced supply meets increased demand. These events are often considered catalysts for new market cycles, with each halving leading to a reduction in the rate of inflation and, in turn, a potential increase in price.

Understanding Bitcoin's market cycles is essential for investors and stakeholders in the cryptocurrency ecosystem. Recognizing the cyclical nature of Bitcoin's price movements can help investors make more informed decisions, manage risk, and avoid falling prey to irrational exuberance or panic during extreme market conditions.

Long-term investors often use market cycles as a guide for accumulating Bitcoin during periods of consolidation or correction when prices are relatively lower. This strategy, known as dollar-cost averaging, entails investing a fixed amount at regular intervals, reducing the impact of short-term price fluctuations.

Traders and speculators, on the other hand, may attempt to capitalize on short-term price movements by leveraging technical analysis and market sentiment indicators. However, trading in a highly volatile market like Bitcoin carries significant risks and requires a deep understanding of market dynamics.

Recognizing market cycles for the broader cryptocurrency industry can inform strategic decisions, project development, and resource allocation. Understanding the macro trends and market sentiment can help projects and startups navigate the ever-changing cryptocurrency landscape and adapt to shifting market conditions.

While market cycles and supply and demand dynamics play a significant role in Bitcoin's price fluctuations, other external factors also influence its value. Both positive and negative regulatory developments can impact investor sentiment and market confidence. Favorable regulatory measures can increase institutional adoption and investor participation, while unfavorable regulations may have the opposite effect.

Moreover, macroeconomic trends and geopolitical events can spill over into the cryptocurrency markets. For instance, economic uncertainty or currency devaluation in a specific region may drive increased interest in With Bitcoin, you can protect yourself from inflation and unstable economies.

Media coverage and public perception of Bitcoin can also influence its price movements. Positive news stories or endorsements from influential figures may boost investor confidence, while negative coverage or FUD (fear, uncertainty, and doubt) can lead to short-term sell-offs.

Bitcoin's price fluctuations and market cycles are intrinsic to its nature as a decentralized and volatile asset. The absence of a central authority governing its price, coupled with its fixed supply and nascent market, contributes to its dramatic price movements.

Understanding Bitcoin's market cycles can provide valuable insights for investors and stakeholders, enabling them to make informed decisions, manage risk, and navigate the ever-changing cryptocurrency landscape. While Bitcoin's price volatility remains a characteristic of the cryptocurrency, its underlying technology and the broader blockchain ecosystem continue to drive innovation, transforming the future of finance and decentralized technologies.

Chapter VII
Bitcoin's Impact on the Financial World

Disrupting traditional financial institutions

The pioneering cryptocurrency introduced in 2009, Bitcoin, has emerged as a disruptive force that challenges traditional financial institutions and the conventional monetary system. This section explores how Bitcoin's decentralized nature, borderless transactions, and potential to provide financial services to the unbanked have reshaped the finance landscape and prompted traditional institutions to reassess their role in the digital age. From the implications of central bank digital currencies (CBDCs) to the rise of decentralized finance (DeFi), Bitcoin's disruptive influence is driving innovation and redefining the future of finance.

At the core of Bitcoin's disruptive potential is its decentralized nature. Unlike traditional financial systems, which rely on central authorities like banks and governments to manage and control transactions, Bitcoin operates on a decentralized blockchain network. This peer-to-peer network enables direct transactions between users without intermediaries, granting individuals greater financial sovereignty.

The absence of intermediaries means that individuals can conduct cross-border transactions without needing currency conversions or exorbitant fees. This aspect of Bitcoin particularly appeals to those in countries with insufficient access to traditional banking services and financial infrastructure.

Bitcoin's decentralization also challenges traditional financial institutions, as it diminishes their monopolistic hold over financial transactions. With the ability to store and transact value independently, individuals have more control over their wealth, reducing their reliance on centralized institutions for financial services.

Bitcoin's borderless nature empowers individuals to participate in the global economy without the restrictions imposed by traditional financial systems. Anyone with a connection in the internet can access the Bitcoin network and engage in transactions, regardless of geographic location.

For individuals in regions with limited financial infrastructure, Bitcoin offers an alternative means of participating in the global economy and accessing financial services. This inclusivity has significant implications for the unbanked and underbanked populations, who may now have access to a decentralized financial system.

Moreover, Bitcoin's borderless transactions facilitate remittances, enabling individuals to send money to their families and friends in different countries at lower costs than traditional remittance services. This use case has gained traction, particularly for migrant workers seeking to send money back home.

Bitcoin's disruptive potential poses challenges to traditional financial institutions. Centralized banking systems have long been the gatekeepers of the financial ecosystem, acting as intermediaries for transactions and lending. However, with the advent of Bitcoin, individuals can bypass these intermediaries and transact directly with one another.

This disintermediation threatens banks' revenue streams, as they could lose market share in payment processing, remittances, and other financial services. Additionally, as Bitcoin becomes increasingly recognized as a store of value and an alternative investment, it competes with traditional asset classes like gold and government bonds.

Central banks all over the world have been investigating the idea of central bank digital currencies, or CBDCs, in reaction to the disruptive potential presented by cryptocurrencies like Bitcoin. These are virtual currency that are generated and administered by central banks.

The goal of CBDCs is to bring together the advantages of cryptocurrencies—like quick and international transactions—with the security and reliability of conventional fiat money. By providing a government-issued digital currency, central banks seek to retain control over monetary policy and financial stability while addressing some of the shortcomings of traditional banking systems.

However, introducing CBDCs raises important questions about privacy, financial surveillance, and the potential to centralize financial power further. While CBDCs may offer benefits in terms of efficiency and financial inclusion, they also require robust privacy protections to prevent excessive surveillance.

In addition to challenging traditional financial institutions, Bitcoin's disruptive influence extends to the broader realm of decentralized finance (DeFi). DeFi is a rapidly developing ecosystem that leverages blockchain technology to create decentralized, transparent, and open financial services.

DeFi platforms permit users to access financial services like lending, borrowing, trading, and yield farming without relying on traditional banks or intermediaries. This democratization of finance empowers individuals to take control of their assets and participate in the financial ecosystem directly.

Through DeFi, individuals can lend their cryptocurrencies to earn interest, access loans collateralized by digital assets, and trade various financial instruments. These activities occur directly on blockchain networks, without the need for intermediaries.

Bitcoin's disruptive influence has been instrumental in inspiring the development of DeFi, with many DeFi protocols built on Ethereum and other blockchain networks. As DeFi grows and matures, it has the potential to transform traditional financial services, offering greater accessibility, efficiency, and transparency to users worldwide.

As Bitcoin and cryptocurrencies disrupt traditional financial institutions, they also pose regulatory challenges for governments and policymakers. The decentralized and borderless nature of Bitcoin makes it difficult to apply conventional financial regulations, leading to debates about the appropriate legal frameworks for cryptocurrencies.

Some governments have embraced Bitcoin and cryptocurrencies, recognizing their potential for financial inclusion and economic growth. Others have taken a more cautious approach, implementing regulations to address concerns about money laundering, terrorist financing, and consumer protection.

Navigating these regulatory landscapes is crucial for the continued growth of Bitcoin and the cryptocurrency ecosystem. Balancing between innovation and consumer protection is essential to foster a thriving and sustainable digital economy.

Bitcoin's disruptive influence on traditional financial institutions transforms how individuals store, transact, and access financial services. Its decentralized nature grants financial sovereignty to individuals, challenging the dominance of centralized institutions.

By enabling borderless transactions and promoting financial inclusion, Bitcoin empowers individuals in underserved regions and facilitates cross-border remittances. These capabilities have far-reaching implications for financial services and economic development.

As Bitcoin and cryptocurrencies continue to disrupt traditional finance, they also present challenges to governments and policymakers seeking to strike the right balance between innovation and regulation. While central bank digital currencies (CBDCs) and decentralized finance (DeFi) offer potential solutions, the path forward requires thoughtful consideration and stakeholder collaboration.

Overall, Bitcoin's disruptive influence underscores the transformative potential of blockchain technology and the need to reimagine the financial landscape for a more inclusive and accessible digital economy. As the world continues to embrace the benefits of decentralized finance, the legacy of Bitcoin's disruption will shape the future of finance for generations to come.

Role of Bitcoin in remittances and cross-border payments

The very first cryptocurrency, Bitcoin, has been a disruptive force for cross-border payments and remittances. This section explores how Bitcoin's decentralized nature, low transaction costs, and borderless capabilities have revolutionized the traditional remittance industry. From enabling faster and more affordable cross-border transactions to empowering individuals in underserved regions, Bitcoin's role in remittances is reshaping the global financial landscape and providing new opportunities for financial inclusion.

Traditional remittance services have long been the primary means for individuals to send money across borders to support their families and loved ones. However, these services are often associated with high fees, lengthy processing times, and limited accessibility.

Sending money through traditional remittance channels can involve multiple intermediaries, each adding their fees and currency conversion costs. This results in a significant reduction in the amount received by the recipient, especially in regions where remittance fees can be as high as 10% or more.

Moreover, the time it takes for the funds to reach the recipient can be several days or even weeks. This delay can be particularly challenging for individuals needing financial assistance.

Traditional remittances' high costs and inefficiencies have prompted many to seek alternative solutions that offer faster, cheaper, and more accessible cross-border transactions.

Bitcoin's decentralized nature and borderless capabilities make it an attractive alternative for cross-border payments. As a digital currency, Bitcoin can be sent directly from one user to another without intermediaries or currency conversions.

The borderless nature of Bitcoin transactions means that individuals can send money to any part of the world with minimal friction. This is especially beneficial for individuals in regions with insufficient access to traditional banking services or those facing economic instability and currency restrictions.

Additionally, Bitcoin transactions typically involve lower fees compared to traditional remittance services. The absence of intermediaries and the decentralized nature of the Bitcoin network contribute to reduced transaction costs, making it a cost-effective option for cross-border payments.

One of the most significant impacts of Bitcoin in remittances is its potential to provide financial inclusion to the unbanked and underbanked populations. In many regions, individuals lack access to formal banking systems, making sending and receiving remittances through traditional channels challenging.

With Bitcoin, all that is needed is a smartphone or computer with internet access, enabling even those without a traditional bank account to participate in cross-border transactions. This inclusivity empowers individuals in underserved regions and gives them greater control over their financial resources.

Furthermore, Bitcoin's borderless transactions can potentially bridge the financial divide between developed and developing economies. Individuals in countries with more robust financial infrastructures can send money to their families in regions with weaker systems, directly supporting economic development and poverty alleviation.

Bitcoin's ability to facilitate near-instant transactions is another key advantage for remittances. Traditional remittance services often involve multiple layers of intermediaries, each contributing to longer processing times. With Bitcoin, transactions can be fulfilled in minutes, regardless of the sender's and recipient's locations.

The speed and efficiency of Bitcoin transactions are particularly beneficial during emergencies or situations requiring urgent financial assistance. By eliminating delays, Bitcoin helps provide timely support to needy individuals, such as disaster relief efforts or medical emergencies.

While Bitcoin's low fees and fast transactions are advantageous, its price volatility can pose challenges for cross-border payments. The value of Bitcoin can experience significant fluctuations over short periods, potentially resulting in variations in the amount received by the recipient.

Some remittance services and individuals use hedging strategies to mitigate the impact of price volatility. Hedging involves converting Bitcoin to the recipient's local currency immediately after receiving it, reducing exposure to Bitcoin's price fluctuations.

Additionally, various financial products and services have emerged to manage the risks associated with Bitcoin price volatility. These include stablecoins, which are cryptocurrencies pegged to the value of fiat currencies, offering a more stable medium for cross-border payments.

As Bitcoin's role in remittances and cross-border payments continues to expand, it has prompted regulatory and legal considerations for governments and policymakers. The decentralized nature of Bitcoin makes it challenging to apply traditional financial regulations, leading to ongoing discussions about the appropriate legal frameworks for cryptocurrencies.

Some countries have embraced Bitcoin and cryptocurrencies, recognizing their potential for financial inclusion and economic growth. Others have taken a more cautious approach, implementing regulations to address concerns about money laundering, terrorist financing, and consumer protection.

Navigating these regulatory landscapes is essential for the continued growth of Bitcoin in the remittance industry. Balancing innovation and consumer protection is crucial to foster a thriving and sustainable digital economy.

While Bitcoin has shown great potential in transforming cross-border payments, it is worth noting that it may not entirely replace traditional remittance services in the near term. Many individuals still rely on traditional remittance providers' familiarity and established networks.

Complementary solutions that bridge the gap between Bitcoin and traditional remittances are emerging. For example, some remittance services use blockchain technology to refine the transparency and efficiency of cross-border transactions without fully adopting Bitcoin or other cryptocurrencies.

Additionally, partnerships between traditional financial institutions and cryptocurrency platforms are being explored to offer seamless and cost-effective cross-border payment solutions. These partnerships seek to leverage the strengths of both traditional banking systems and blockchain technology to provide more accessible and efficient remittance services.

Bitcoin's role in remittances and cross-border payments is disrupting the traditional remittance industry by offering borderless, low-cost, and fast transactions. Its decentralized nature empowers individuals with financial sovereignty and provides new opportunities for financial inclusion.

While challenges remain in terms of regulatory considerations and price volatility, Bitcoin's transformative influence on cross-border transactions is reshaping the global financial landscape. By providing an alternative to traditional remittance services, Bitcoin is facilitating financial empowerment, economic development, and greater accessibility to financial services for individuals worldwide. As the world continues to embrace the potential of digital currencies, the impact of Bitcoin's role in remittances will continue to shape the future of cross-border payments for generations to come.

Bitcoin: A store of value and hedge against inflation

Bitcoin, the first cryptocurrency created in 2009, has garnered attention as a potential store of value and hedge against inflation. This section explores the characteristics that make Bitcoin an attractive store of value, how it compares to traditional stores of value like gold, and its potential as a hedge against the erosive effects of inflation. As global economic uncertainties persist and central banks implement expansionary monetary policies, the role of Bitcoin as a digital asset with scarcity and decentralization is redefining the concept of store of value and reshaping investment strategies.

A store of value is an asset that maintains its purchasing power over time and serves as a reliable repository of wealth. Traditional stores of value, such as gold and other precious metals, have been historically favored for their scarcity, durability, and intrinsic value. These assets have acted as hedges against economic instability and currency devaluation.

Bitcoin shares some key characteristics with traditional stores of value, making it a contender in the digital age. Firstly, Bitcoin's supply is capped at 21 million coins, a feature embedded in its code. This scarcity sharply contrasts fiat currencies, which can be printed by central banks without limit, leading to potential devaluation over time.

Secondly, Bitcoin's decentralized nature, operating on a global peer-to-peer network, means that no central authority can manipulate its value or control its distribution. This decentralization enhances its appeal as a store of value, as it is less susceptible to political or institutional interference.

Additionally, the durability and fungibility of Bitcoin contribute to its store of value potential. Its digital nature ensures that it can be stored securely and transferred easily across borders, making it a practical option for those seeking to preserve wealth and access financial services in the digital age.

Gold has long been considered the ultimate store of value and a hedge against economic uncertainties. Its physical properties, scarcity, and historical value as a medium of exchange have made it a trusted asset for wealth preservation.

Bitcoin's emergence as a digital store of value has drawn comparisons to gold, with proponents dubbing it "digital gold." Both assets exhibit scarcity, and Bitcoin's fixed supply algorithm is often likened to the finite nature of gold reserves.

However, there are fundamental differences between Bitcoin and gold. While gold is a tangible commodity with practical applications in industries such as jewelry and electronics, Bitcoin is a purely digital asset. Its value is derived from its properties as a secure, decentralized, and scarce form of money.

Another key distinction lies in the historical role of gold as a store of value for millennia, while Bitcoin is a relatively new asset with just over a decade of existence. Gold's enduring reputation as a store of value gives it a sense of stability and trust that Bitcoin is still striving to establish.

Yet, Bitcoin's portability, divisibility, and ease of transfer offer unique benefits in the digital era. Its global accessibility and ability to function as a store of value beyond geographical boundaries make it attractive to a growing cohort of investors and users.

Inflation, the increase in the overall price level of goods and services over time, erodes the purchasing power of fiat currencies. As central banks implement expansionary monetary policies, printing more money to stimulate economic growth, concerns about potential inflationary pressures grow.

Due to its fixed supply algorithm, Bitcoin's scarcity makes it an attractive hedge against inflation. In contrast to fiat currencies, which are susceptible to an infinite increase in the money supply, Bitcoin's capped supply ensures that new coins are issued at a predictable and decreasing rate until the 21 millionth coin is mined.

The idea of Bitcoin as a hedge against inflation draws parallels to gold's function during economic uncertainty. Historically, gold has acted as a safe haven asset during periods of inflationary pressure, providing investors with a store of value that retains its worth amidst depreciating fiat currencies.

Bitcoin's relatively short history and recent adoption as a store of value means that its role as an inflation hedge is still being tested and debated. The cryptocurrency has experienced significant price volatility, which can challenge its perception as a stable store of value.

Additionally, Bitcoin's correlation with traditional financial markets during times of economic turbulence raises questions about its independence as a safe haven asset. As the cryptocurrency market matures, its performance will be scrutinized during economic downturns and inflationary environments.

The idea of Bitcoin as a store of value and hedge against inflation has prompted some investors and institutions to incorporate the cryptocurrency into their investment strategies. As part of a diversified portfolio, Bitcoin's unique properties can complement traditional asset classes and offer potential benefits during economic uncertainties.

Traditional investment portfolios typically include a mix of stocks, bonds, and commodities. Adding Bitcoin to this combination introduces a digital asset that behaves differently from traditional financial instruments. This diversification can reduce overall portfolio risk and increase potential returns.

For some institutional investors, Bitcoin serves as a portfolio diversifier and an allocation to an emerging asset class with significant growth potential. As the world shifts toward digital economies and blockchain technologies, exposure to cryptocurrencies becomes a strategic consideration for long-term investment strategies.

While Bitcoin's role as a store of value and hedge against inflation is gaining recognition, it is not without challenges and risks. Price volatility remains a defining feature of the cryptocurrency market, and investors must be prepared for significant price fluctuations.

Furthermore, regulatory developments and legal uncertainties can impact the cryptocurrency ecosystem, leading to potential risks for investors and users. The regulatory landscape for cryptocurrencies is developing, and regulation changes can influence investor sentiment and market dynamics.

Additionally, the developing nature of Bitcoin and the cryptocurrency market means that the asset class is subject to market sentiment, speculative activity, and technological advancements. As with any investment, due diligence and risk management are essential for individuals and institutions considering exposure to Bitcoin.

Bitcoin's emergence as a store of value and hedge against inflation marks a significant shift in the financial landscape. Its scarcity, decentralization, and digital nature provide unique properties that resonate with a growing cohort of investors seeking alternatives to traditional stores of value.

While comparisons to gold and other traditional assets are drawn, Bitcoin's digital form and relatively short history distinguish it as a novel investment opportunity. The role of Bitcoin as a store of value and hedge against inflation is still being explored, and its long-term implications for the global economy and financial markets continue to unfold.

As global economic uncertainties persist and technology reshapes the world of finance, Bitcoin's unique characteristics position it as a contender in the evolving concept of wealth preservation. Whether Bitcoin will solidify its place as a reliable store of value and inflation hedge remains to be seen, but its disruptive influence on the financial landscape is undeniable. As the world embraces digital currencies and blockchain technologies, Bitcoin's role as a transformative asset class will continue to shape the future of investment strategies and financial inclusion for generations to come.

Chapter VIII
Regulatory Challenges and Legal Status

Governments' responses to Bitcoin

The rise of Bitcoin, the pioneering cryptocurrency introduced in 2009, has presented governments worldwide with a new and unique set of challenges and opportunities. As a decentralized digital currency operating on a global peer-to-peer network, Bitcoin disrupts traditional financial systems and raises questions about regulation, taxation, financial stability, and national sovereignty. This section explores how governments have responded to the emergence of Bitcoin, including varying approaches to regulation, concerns about illicit use, exploration of central bank digital currencies (CBDCs), and recognition of blockchain technology's potential for innovation and economic growth.

The decentralized nature of Bitcoin, operating outside the control of traditional financial institutions, has prompted governments to develop regulatory frameworks to address concerns about money laundering, terrorist financing, and consumer protection. The approach to regulation varies significantly from country to country, with some governments embracing cryptocurrencies, others adopting a cautious approach, and some instituting outright bans.

Countries such as Japan, Switzerland, and Singapore have established clear legal frameworks for cryptocurrency exchanges, requiring them to comply with strict anti-money laundering (or AML) and know-your-customer (KYC) requirements. These regulatory measures aim to protect investors and users while fostering a conducive environment for cryptocurrency innovation.

On the other hand, countries like China and India have taken a more restrictive approach, implementing bans or placing severe restrictions on cryptocurrency-related activities. In these cases, the concern is often linked to potential risks to financial stability and the potential for illicit use.

The United States, being a significant player in the global cryptocurrency market, has also grappled with regulatory challenges. Regulatory clarity and consistency remain ongoing concerns, with various regulatory bodies overseeing different aspects of the cryptocurrency ecosystem.

The pseudonymous nature of Bitcoin transactions has led to concerns about its potential application for illegal activities, like money laundering, tax evasion, and illicit transactions on the dark web. Governments have responded by implementing AML and KYC requirements on cryptocurrency exchanges and businesses.

Financial Action Task Force (or FATF), an international body responsible for setting global AML standards, has issued guidelines to combat money laundering and terrorist financing in cryptocurrency. These guidelines require exchanges and other virtual asset service providers to collect and share customer information to enhance transparency and traceability.

While regulatory efforts are aimed at curbing illicit use, it is essential to balance consumer protection and maintaining the privacy and decentralization principles underpinning Bitcoin's appeal.

The emergence of cryptocurrencies like Bitcoin has prompted some central banks to explore the concept of CBDCs. A CBDC is a digital national currency issued and regulated by a central bank. The potential benefits of CBDCs include faster and more efficient payment systems, increased financial inclusion, and enhanced monetary policy tools.

Countries like China and Sweden have been at the forefront of CBDC development and trials. The People's Bank of China (or PBOC) has been conducting pilot programs for its digital yuan, aiming to digitize the national currency and enhance financial inclusion. Similarly, the Riksbank in Sweden has been exploring the issuance of an e-krona to address the decline in the use of cash.

CBDCs allow governments to leverage blockchain technology for national currencies while retaining control over monetary policy and financial stability. However, introducing CBDCs raises important questions about privacy, financial surveillance, and the potential to centralize financial power further.

While some governments have been cautious about cryptocurrencies, many have recognized the potential of blockchain technology for innovation and economic growth. Blockchain, Bitcoin's underlying technology, is a decentralized and immutable ledger that can facilitate secure and transparent transactions across various industries.

Governments are exploring the use of blockchain for applications beyond cryptocurrencies. These applications include supply chain management, voting systems, identity verification, land registry, and intellectual property protection.

By embracing blockchain technology, governments seek to improve efficiency, reduce fraud, and enhance transparency in various sectors. Using blockchain for government services can also save costs and increase trust between citizens and institutions.

The taxation of cryptocurrencies is another aspect that governments have grappled with as Bitcoin and other cryptocurrencies gain popularity. Taxation guidelines for cryptocurrencies vary significantly from country to country, with some treating them as commodities, others as property, and some as currency.

The taxation of cryptocurrency transactions involves complexities, especially considering the pseudonymous nature of Bitcoin. Governments are developing guidelines to ensure that individuals and businesses accurately report their cryptocurrency-related income and capital gains.

Cryptocurrency tax guidelines often cover various scenarios, such as mining, trading, and using cryptocurrencies for goods and services. Tax authorities continually update their guidelines as the cryptocurrency market evolves to adapt to changing circumstances.

The response of governments to Bitcoin and other cryptocurrencies is critical in defining the role of digital assets in the global economy and shaping the future of financial systems. As technology advances and economic landscapes shift, the impact of governments' responses on the digital financial ecosystem will continue to unfold.

In conclusion, the emergence of Bitcoin and other cryptocurrencies has presented governments with unique challenges and opportunities. The decentralized nature of Bitcoin has prompted regulatory efforts to address concerns about illicit use and consumer protection. Governments worldwide have adopted varying approaches to regulation, ranging from embracing cryptocurrencies to imposing restrictions and bans.

The rise of Bitcoin has also sparked exploration into central bank digital currencies, as countries seek to leverage blockchain technology for national currencies and enhance financial inclusion. While CBDCs present new opportunities, they also raise questions about privacy and financial surveillance.

Blockchain technology, the underlying innovation behind Bitcoin, has been recognized for its potential in various sectors beyond cryptocurrencies. Governments are exploring its applications for supply chain management, voting systems, identity verification, and more.

The taxation of cryptocurrencies is an ongoing concern for governments, as they strive to develop guidelines to accurately address the complexities of reporting cryptocurrency-related income and capital gains.

Overall, the response of governments to Bitcoin is a multifaceted and evolving process. As the world embraces digital currencies and blockchain technologies, the impact of governments' actions will continue to shape the future of finance and digital economies for generations to come.

Legal considerations for Bitcoin users and businesses

The increasing adoption of Bitcoin, the pioneering cryptocurrency, has brought forth a myriad of legal considerations for users and businesses alike. As a decentralized virtual asset operating on a global scale, Bitcoin's unique characteristics challenge existing legal frameworks, prompting governments and regulatory bodies to grapple with issues related to taxation, consumer protection, money laundering, and more. This section delves into the legal complexities Bitcoin users and businesses face, exploring the evolving regulatory landscape, compliance challenges, and the need for balanced and clear legal guidelines to foster innovation while protecting stakeholders.

One of the primary legal considerations for Bitcoin users and businesses is taxation. The treatment of Bitcoin for tax purposes varies from country to country, and often within different jurisdictions within the same country. Governments are grappling with classifying Bitcoin as a currency, commodity, or property for taxation purposes. In some countries, Bitcoin transactions are subject to capital gains tax, similar to the taxation of stocks or real estate. When users and businesses buy, sell, or exchange Bitcoin, they may be required to report their gains or losses to the tax authorities. For businesses, accepting Bitcoin as payment for goods and services can introduce accounting and tax reporting complexities. The fluctuating value of Bitcoin poses challenges in calculating the equivalent fiat currency value for tax purposes, as the value of Bitcoin can change between the time of the transaction and the time of reporting.

Complying with anti-money laundering (AML) and know-your-customer (KYC) regulations is another crucial legal consideration for Bitcoin users and businesses. Regulators aim to prevent the illicit use of cryptocurrencies for money laundering, terrorist financing, and other illegal activities. Bitcoin exchanges and businesses facilitating cryptocurrency transactions are often subject to stringent AML/KYC requirements. This includes collecting and verifying customer information, monitoring transactions for doubtful activities, and reporting any suspicious transactions to the relevant authorities. The decentralized and pseudonymous nature of Bitcoin transactions presents challenges for regulators in ensuring compliance. However, governments are developing guidelines and standards to address these concerns and promote a more transparent and accountable cryptocurrency ecosystem.

The increasing use of Bitcoin for online purchases and financial transactions raises consumer protection and security questions. Unlike traditional payment systems, Bitcoin transactions are irreversible, and users must exercise caution when sending funds to prevent loss or fraud. Bitcoin's pseudonymous nature also means that users may not have the same recourse as they do with traditional financial institutions if they fall victim to scams or fraudulent activities. In this regard, governments are exploring ways to enhance consumer protection for Bitcoin users, such as through education and awareness campaigns and providing resources for dispute resolution. Furthermore, the security of Bitcoin wallets and storage solutions is crucial. Users and businesses must take measures to protect their private keys and funds from unauthorized access or hacking attempts.

Bitcoin's borderless nature poses challenges for regulatory authorities in different jurisdictions. The global nature of the cryptocurrency market means that users and businesses can transact with individuals and entities from different countries, potentially leading to conflicts of laws and regulatory discrepancies. Jurisdictional challenges are particularly evident in cases involving fraudulent activities, hacks, or other criminal acts that cross international borders. The lack of a central authority overseeing Bitcoin transactions can complicate efforts to investigate and prosecute such activities. Governments are working on international cooperation and coordination to address cross-border issues related to Bitcoin and cryptocurrencies. Initiatives like the Financial Action Task Force (or FATF) seek to develop global standards and best practices for regulating cryptocurrencies and combating illicit activities.

Blockchain, as the underlying technology behind Bitcoin, has far-reaching applications beyond cryptocurrencies. Blockchain technology is being explored for various uses, including supply chain management, intellectual property protection, and decentralized applications (DApps). Legal considerations related to blockchain technology include intellectual property rights for innovations and inventions built on blockchain. Governments and businesses are navigating issues related to patenting blockchain-based technologies and resolving disputes over ownership and licensing rights. Additionally, using blockchain for data storage and validation raises questions about data privacy and compliance with data protection laws. As blockchain technology becomes more prevalent, governments are exploring ways to ensure data security and privacy in decentralized systems.

Initial coin offerings (ICOs) have emerged as a popular fundraising mechanism for blockchain projects. ICOs involve the issuance of tokens or digital assets in exchange for funding to develop a project or platform. The legal status of ICOs has been a subject of debate and regulatory scrutiny. Depending on the certain features of the tokens and the fundraising model, ICOs may be classified as securities offerings, subjecting them to securities regulation. Regulators in various countries are working to establish guidelines and standards for ICOs to protect investors and ensure transparency in fundraising activities. The legal landscape for ICOs is still evolving, and businesses engaging in token sales must navigate these regulations to avoid potential legal pitfalls.

Tax implications of using Bitcoin

There are now a lot of people using Bitcoin and other cryptocurrencies as investment and exchange platforms, which has led to significant concerns about the tax implications for both individuals and companies. As a decentralized digital asset, Bitcoin operates outside the control of traditional financial institutions and poses unique challenges for tax authorities worldwide. This section explores the tax implications of using Bitcoin, including taxation of transactions, capital gains, reporting obligations, regulatory developments, and the need for clarity in tax guidelines to ensure compliance and foster the responsible use of cryptocurrencies.

The tax treatment of Bitcoin transactions varies from country to country, as tax authorities grapple with classifying cryptocurrencies. Some jurisdictions treat Bitcoin as a currency, subjecting it to regular income tax rules for transactions involving goods and services. In such cases, individuals and businesses must report gains or losses from Bitcoin transactions as part of their taxable income. On the other hand, some countries treat Bitcoin as property or a commodity, resulting in taxation similar to that of capital gains on investments. When using Bitcoin to purchase goods or services, individuals are typically required to calculate the value of the transaction in fiat currency at the time of the transaction. The difference between the purchase price and the current value of Bitcoin at the time of the transaction determines the taxable gain or loss. For businesses that accept Bitcoin as payment, the value of goods or services sold in Bitcoin must be converted to the fiat currency equivalent for tax reporting purposes.

Bitcoin's volatility and potential for significant price appreciation have made it an attractive investment option. As with other investments, capital gains tax applies to profits made from selling or exchanging Bitcoin at a higher value than its acquisition cost. The tax rate for capital gains on Bitcoin investments varies depending on the holding period and the individual's overall income level. Short-term capital gains, coming from the sale of Bitcoin held for less than a specified period (usually one year in many jurisdictions), are typically taxed at the individual's regular income tax rate. On the other hand, long-term capital gains, arising from the sale of Bitcoin held for more than the specified period, often qualify for preferential tax rates, generally lower than regular income tax rates.

Tax reporting obligations for Bitcoin users can be complex, especially considering the pseudonymous nature of cryptocurrency transactions. Tax authorities often require individuals to maintain detailed records of their Bitcoin transactions, including dates of acquisitions, sale prices, and any relevant expenses incurred during the process. For businesses, accepting Bitcoin payments adds another layer of reporting complexity. They must accurately document each transaction's details, including the value of the goods or services sold in fiat currency at the time of the transaction. Compliance with tax regulations can be challenging, particularly for individuals and businesses conducting a high volume of Bitcoin transactions. Failure to accurately report cryptocurrency transactions may lead to penalties, audits, and potential legal repercussions. Some jurisdictions have introduced specific guidelines for calculating and reporting cryptocurrency-related income and capital gains to facilitate compliance.

As the cryptocurrency market continues to evolve, tax authorities worldwide are working to adapt their regulations to address the unique challenges of cryptocurrencies like Bitcoin. Regulatory developments aim to clarify tax guidelines, foster compliance, and prevent tax evasion. International cooperation and coordination have become crucial as cryptocurrencies transcend national borders. The lack of a central governing authority for cryptocurrencies necessitates collaborative efforts among governments to establish global standards for taxation. Initiatives such as the OECD's Base Erosion and Profit Shifting (BEPS) project seek to address tax challenges posed by the digital economy, including cryptocurrencies.

The quickly changing landscape of the cryptocurrency market can lead to uncertainty regarding tax implications. Cryptocurrency users and businesses may struggle to keep up with evolving tax regulations and interpretations. Clarity and consistency in tax guidelines are essential to promote responsible use of Bitcoin and other cryptocurrencies. Governments need to provide clear definitions of how cryptocurrencies are classified for tax purposes and clear instructions on reporting obligations and applicable tax rates. This will help users and businesses confidently navigate the tax landscape, fostering a more transparent and compliant cryptocurrency ecosystem.

Bitcoin mining, the procedure of validating transactions and adding them to the blockchain, is essential to the cryptocurrency network's functioning. Individuals and businesses engaged in mining activities are generally subject to income tax on the value of the mined Bitcoin at the time of receipt. Staking, which involves actively participating in a proof-of-stake blockchain network, is another method of earning cryptocurrency rewards. Tax treatment for staking varies by jurisdiction, with some countries considering staking rewards as taxable income when received, while others treat them as capital gains when the staked cryptocurrency is eventually sold.

Hard forks, which result in the creation of new cryptocurrencies from the original blockchain, and airdrops, where users receive new tokens as a giveaway, can have tax implications for users. The tax treatment of hard forks and airdrops depends on individual tax regulations, with some countries considering them as taxable events when the new tokens are received or sold.

Chapter IX
Bitcoin Mining and Energy Consumption

How mining contributes to the network

Bitcoin mining, a crucial aspect of the cryptocurrency's functioning, is vital in maintaining the integrity of the network and validating transactions. Mining is a competitive and resource-intensive process that involves solving complex mathematical puzzles to add new blocks to the blockchain. This section explores the essential contributions of mining to the Bitcoin network, including transaction validation, security, consensus mechanism, issuance of new bitcoins, and the challenges and environmental impact associated with mining.

At the core of Bitcoin mining is the process of validating transactions and including them in new blocks. A Bitcoin transaction that a user starts is released to the network and added to the mempool, which is a collection of unprocessed transactions. Miners take transactions out of the mempool and add them to freshly created blocks that are appended to the blockchain. There is a restriction on how many transactions can fit into each block, so miners have to compete to get the network to accept their blocks.

Proof-of-Work (PoW) is a cryptographic puzzle that miners must solve in order to verify transactions as well as generate new blocks. This involves finding a nonce (a random number) that, when combined with the transactions in the block and the previous block's hash, produces a hash that meets specific criteria (e.g., starts with a certain number of leading zeros). This process is computationally intensive and requires substantial computing power.

Mining contributes significantly to the security of the Bitcoin network. By solving the PoW puzzle, miners demonstrate that they have invested computational power in creating a block. This investment deters malicious actors seeking to alter past transactions or create fraudulent blocks.

In a PoW-based system like Bitcoin, an attacker would need to control most of the network's computational power (known as a 51% attack) to have a realistic chance of altering the blockchain's history. Achieving such control is highly improbable due to the decentralized nature of mining. The widespread distribution of mining nodes worldwide makes it challenging for any single entity to gain control over the network.

As a result, the Bitcoin network has demonstrated high security since its inception, providing confidence to users and businesses that their transactions are protected against manipulation and fraud.

Bitcoin mining is essential on the network's consensus mechanism. As miners compete to solve the PoW puzzle and create new blocks, they are simultaneously working to achieve a consensus on the validity of transactions. Once a miner successfully solves the puzzle and creates a block, it is broadcast to the network for verification.

Other nodes in the network then validate the new block's contents and confirm that the PoW solution is valid. Consensus is achieved when most nodes agree on the validity of the new block. This consensus mechanism ensures that all nodes in the network share the same version of the blockchain and agree on the order of transactions.

The confirmation process provides finality to transactions, reducing the risk of double-spending and ensuring that all participants in the network have a consistent view of the state of the blockchain.

Another critical function of mining is the issuance of new bitcoins. As a reward for their efforts in creating new blocks and securing the network, miners receive a certain quantity of newly minted bitcoins and transaction fees paid by users. This process is often referred to as the "block reward."

The block reward in the early days of Bitcoin was fifty bitcoins. However, the block reward is reduced by half roughly every four years as part of the monetary policy incorporated into Bitcoin. This event is known as the "halving," occurring every 210,000 blocks. As of the most recent halving in 2020, the block reward is 6.25 bitcoins per block.

The controlled issuance of new bitcoins through mining is a key feature of Bitcoin's monetary policy, designed to create scarcity and avoid hyperinflation. The gradual reduction in the block reward over time means that the total supply of bitcoins is fixed to 21 million, making it a deflationary asset.

While mining plays a crucial role in the Bitcoin network, it also faces several challenges, including scalability and energy consumption. As the number of transactions on the network grows, miners must process a higher volume of transactions within each block. This can lead to congestion in the mempool and longer transaction confirmation times.

To address scalability challenges, developers and researchers are exploring potential solutions, such as the Lightning Network, which aims to enable faster and more cost-effective off-chain transactions.

One of the most significant criticisms of Bitcoin mining is its energy consumption. The computational power required to solve the PoW puzzle demands considerable electricity. Large-scale mining operations are often located in regions with cheap electricity, which can lead to concerns about environmental impact and carbon emissions.

Efforts are underway to make Bitcoin mining more energy-efficient and environmentally friendly. Some mining operations are exploring the utilization of renewable energy sources, like the hydroelectric or solar power, to power their mining rigs. Additionally, research is ongoing to develop alternative consensus mechanisms, such as Proof-of-Stake (PoS), requiring less energy than PoW.

Environmental concerns and the push for sustainable mining

As the popularity of cryptocurrencies, particularly Bitcoin, has surged in recent years, so too have concerns about their environmental impact. Bitcoin mining, the process of creating new coins and validating transactions, requires significant computational power and electricity. This has led to a growing awareness of the environmental consequences of mining activities. This section examines the environmental concerns surrounding Bitcoin mining and explores the efforts and innovations aimed at promoting sustainable mining practices.

One of the significant environmental concerns associated with Bitcoin mining is its energy consumption. The mining process entails solving complex mathematical puzzles through the Proof-of-Work (PoW) algorithm. Miners compete to find the right solution, and the winner can add a new block to the blockchain and acquire the block reward in the form of newly minted bitcoins.

The computational power required to perform these calculations demands substantial electricity. Large-scale mining operations, often concentrated in regions with access to cheap electricity, can consume vast amounts of energy. This directly impacts carbon emissions, as many power plants rely on fossil fuels as their primary energy source.

As a result, the carbon footprint of Bitcoin mining has drawn criticism from environmentalists and policymakers concerned about its contribution to climate change. The carbon emissions associated with mining have raised questions about the long-term sustainability of the cryptocurrency industry.

Another environmental concern associated with Bitcoin mining is generating electronic waste or e-waste. The specialized hardware used in mining, such as Application-Specific Integrated Circuits (ASICs), requires frequent upgrades to maintain competitiveness. As newer, more efficient mining equipment is developed, older models become obsolete and are discarded.

The disposal of e-waste can have detrimental effects on the environment, as it often contains hazardous materials that can contaminate the soil and water if not properly managed. The responsible recycling and disposal of mining equipment have become essential considerations for promoting sustainability in the industry.

The concentration of mining operations in certain regions can have localized environmental impacts. In regions with prevalent mining activities, there may be increased pressure on local energy infrastructure and natural resources. This can lead to resource depletion, habitat disruption, and strained water supplies.

Moreover, the influx of miners to specific regions may drive up real estate prices and cause other social and economic challenges. The environmental consequences of such concentration underscore the need for a more geographically diverse and decentralized mining network.

The environmental concerns surrounding Bitcoin mining have spurred a growing movement towards sustainable solutions. One of the most promising approaches is using renewable energy sources to power mining operations.

Some mining companies and individual miners have sought to locate their operations near renewable energy sources, such as hydroelectric, solar, or wind power. By utilizing clean energy sources, these miners aim to reduce the effect on the environment of their operations and reduce their carbon footprint.

Additionally, some mining facilities have been set up in areas with excess renewable energy capacity, effectively using the surplus energy that would otherwise go to waste. This approach promotes sustainability and creates economic opportunities in regions with abundant renewable energy resources.

Innovation in hardware design is another avenue being explored to improve the sustainability of Bitcoin mining. Researchers and manufacturers are working on creating a more energy-efficient mining equipment, reducing the power consumption required for mining operations.

Efforts are being made to optimize the mining process and increase the hash rate per unit of electricity consumed. This can significantly reduce energy usage while maintaining or improving mining efficiency.

A fundamental change being considered to address the environmental concerns of Bitcoin mining is the transition from the current Proof-of-

Work consensus mechanism to Proof-of-Stake (PoS). Unlike PoW, which requires miners to compete and use computational power to validate transactions and create new blocks, PoS selects validators to create new blocks depending on the number of coins they hold and are prepared to "stake" as collateral.

Since PoS does not require energy-intensive calculations, it is considered to be much more energy-efficient and environmentally friendly. By market capitalization, Ethereum is the second-largest cryptocurrency and it has already transitioned to PoS with Ethereum 2.0, which aims to address the energy consumption challenges posed by PoW.

The cryptocurrency community is increasingly aware of the importance of sustainability in mining operations. Several initiatives and organizations have been established to promote sustainable mining practices and provide certifications for environmentally responsible mining.

For example, the Crypto Climate Accord is an industry-led initiative committed to making the cryptocurrency sector 100% renewable by 2025. By bringing together industry stakeholders, this initiative aims to solve the environmental impact of cryptocurrency mining through collective action and collaboration.

Governments worldwide are also beginning to take steps to find a solution for the environmental impact of Bitcoin mining. Some countries have introduced regulations or imposed restrictions on mining operations, especially those reliant on fossil fuel-based energy sources.

On the other hand, several governments are providing incentives and tax breaks to miners using renewable energy sources. By supporting sustainable mining practices, governments aim to balance fostering technological innovation and safeguarding the environment.

Raising awareness among miners and cryptocurrency users about the environmental impact of mining is crucial for promoting sustainable practices. Education initiatives can highlight the benefits of renewable energy and energy-efficient hardware and encourage miners to adopt more sustainable approaches.

Furthermore, promoting transparency and providing accessible information about the environmental impact of different mining practices can help users make environmentally conscious choices when engaging with cryptocurrencies.

Chapter X
Altcoins and the Cryptocurrency Ecosystem

Introduction to altcoins and their differences from Bitcoin

Bitcoin, the first and most well-known cryptocurrency, paved the way for a vast ecosystem of digital currencies that followed. These alternative cryptocurrencies, often called "altcoins," offer unique features, use cases, and technological innovations that differentiate them from Bitcoin. This section introduces altcoins and explores their key differences from Bitcoin, including their consensus mechanisms, transaction speeds, privacy features, supply limits, and community support.

Altcoins, as the name suggests, are alternative cryptocurrencies to Bitcoin. While Bitcoin remains the dominant and most valuable cryptocurrency, thousands of altcoins exist, each with its own distinct characteristics and purposes. Altcoins can be built on different blockchain platforms, such as Ethereum, Binance Smart Chain, or Solana, and they often serve as vehicles for experimenting with new technologies and use cases beyond simple digital currency.

One of the primary differences between altcoins and Bitcoin lies in their consensus mechanisms, the method by which transactions are verified and new blocks are added to the blockchain. Bitcoin relies on the Proof-of-Work (PoW) mechanism, which necessitates miners to solve complicated mathematical puzzles to validate transactions and compete to add new blocks. In contrast, many altcoins use alternative consensus mechanisms like Proof-of-Stake (PoS), Delegated Proof-of-Stake (DPoS), or Practical Byzantine Fault Tolerance (PBFT). PoS-based altcoins select validators based on the number of coins they hold and "stake" as collateral, rather than relying on computational power. These mechanisms offer potential benefits like energy efficiency and increased transaction throughput.

Bitcoin's PoW consensus mechanism has transaction speed and scalability limitations. The Bitcoin blockchain can handle only a limited number of transactions per second, leading to potential network congestion during periods of high demand. This limitation has prompted exploring various scaling solutions, like the Lightning Network, to enable faster and more cost-effective off-chain transactions. Altcoins have sought to address scalability challenges by adopting different consensus mechanisms or implementing Layer 2 solutions. For example, some altcoins leverage DPoS to achieve higher transaction throughput, while others use sharding or sidechains to increase scalability.

Bitcoin's blockchain is transparent, meaning all transactions are publicly recorded and traceable. While Bitcoin addresses do not reveal personal information, analyzing the blockchain and inferring transaction patterns and user behavior is possible. Altcoins have sought to enhance user privacy and anonymity. Some altcoins incorporate privacy-focused features like ring signatures, zero-knowledge proofs, or stealth addresses to obfuscate transaction details and make tracking users' activities on the blockchain harder.

Bitcoin's monetary policy is deflationary, with a fixed supply cap of 21 million bitcoins. The issuance of new bitcoins reduces over time through halving events that occur approximately every four years. This scarcity is intended to make Bitcoin a store of value, akin to precious metals like gold. Altcoins often have different supply limits and inflation models. Some altcoins have a fixed supply, while others have inflationary models that continue to issue new coins over time. The supply dynamics of altcoins can significantly impact their perceived value and utility as digital assets.

Bitcoin's status as the first cryptocurrency has granted it widespread recognition and a significant community following. Its use cases range from a store of value to a hedge against inflation, and it has gained acceptance as a medium of exchange in various industries. Altcoins, on the other hand, often target specific use cases or industries. Some altcoins focus on enabling smart contracts and decentralized applications, while others cater to niche markets or industries, such as supply chain management, identity verification, or non-fungible tokens (NFTs). The level of community support and adoption can vary widely among altcoins. Some altcoins have built vibrant communities and gained substantial market capitalization, while others may struggle to gain traction and face limited use outside of speculative trading.

Altcoins provide a fertile ground for innovation and experimentation in the cryptocurrency space. With the freedom to develop their own consensus mechanisms, supply limits, and features, altcoin creators can explore new ideas and technologies that might not be possible within the confines of the Bitcoin protocol. Some altcoins have introduced novel features like on-chain governance, cross-chain interoperability, or native smart contract functionality. These innovations can drive advancements in the broader blockchain and cryptocurrency ecosystem and inspire further development in the field.

In conclusion, altcoins represent a diverse and dynamic ecosystem of cryptocurrencies that have emerged as alternatives to Bitcoin. They offer various consensus mechanisms, transaction speeds, privacy features, supply limits, and use cases, distinguishing them from the first and most well-known cryptocurrency. While Bitcoin remains the flagship of the cryptocurrency space, altcoins continue to drive innovation and experimentation in the quest for decentralized, efficient, and privacy-centric digital assets.

As the cryptocurrency landscape continues to evolve, the interplay between Bitcoin and altcoins will shape the future of blockchain technology and its potential influence on global finance, commerce, and society. Whether through competition or collaboration, Bitcoin and altcoins together contribute to the ongoing transformation of the financial landscape and the possibilities of decentralized digital currencies.

Major altcoins and their use cases

The rise of altcoins has brought about a diverse array of cryptocurrencies, each with its unique features and use cases. While Bitcoin remains dominant in the cryptocurrency market, many altcoins have emerged to address specific challenges and provide innovative solutions beyond simple digital currency. This section explores some of the major altcoins and their distinctive use cases, including Ethereum, Ripple (XRP), Litecoin, Cardano, and Polkadot.

Altcoins, as the name suggests, are alternative cryptocurrencies to Bitcoin. While Bitcoin remains the dominant and most valuable cryptocurrency, thousands of altcoins exist, each with its own distinct characteristics and purposes. Altcoins can be built on different blockchain platforms, such as Ethereum, Binance Smart Chain, or Solana, and they often serve as vehicles for experimenting with new technologies and use cases beyond simple digital currency.

Ethereum is often regarded as the second most significant cryptocurrency after Bitcoin, primarily due to its pioneering role in introducing smart contracts and decentralized applications (DApps). Unlike Bitcoin, which mainly serves as digital gold and a store of value, Ethereum aims to be a programmable blockchain platform that enables developers to build and deploy DApps.

Developers can create smart contracts—self-executing contracts with predetermined conditions—on the Ethereum network. Numerous applications, including as decentralized finance (DeFi) platforms, non-fungible token (NFT) exchanges, and decentralized autonomous organizations (DAOs), are made possible by these smart contracts.

The flexibility and programmability of Ethereum have contributed to the rapid development of the DeFi sector, where users can access financial services without intermediaries. Additionally, the platform's support for NFTs has revolutionized the art and gaming industries, enabling unique digital assets and ownership verification.

Ripple, represented by the cryptocurrency XRP, focuses on revolutionizing cross-border payments and remittances. Traditional international money transfers can be costly, slow, and subject to intermediaries, resulting in delays and high user fees.

Ripple's blockchain technology aims to provide a seamless and efficient global payments network. It utilizes its unique consensus algorithm, the XRP Ledger (XRPL), which enables fast and low-cost transactions. Through RippleNet, financial institutions can connect and transact directly, reducing the need for correspondent banking relationships and minimizing settlement times.

Ripple's vision of enhancing the traditional financial system's infrastructure and facilitating faster, cheaper cross-border payments has led to partnerships with various financial institutions worldwide. Although Ripple and XRP have faced regulatory challenges, their use case remains focused on improving the global remittance landscape.

Litecoin, or the "silver to Bitcoin's gold," is an early altcoin that shares many similarities with Bitcoin but aims to address certain limitations. Created by Charlie Lee in 2011, Litecoin is a peer-to-peer digital currency that leverages a similar open-source blockchain protocol to Bitcoin.

Litecoin's key differentiators lie in its transaction speed and block generation time. Litecoin's block time is approximately 2.5 minutes, compared to Bitcoin's 10 minutes, enabling faster confirmation of transactions. Litecoin's total supply is four times that of Bitcoin, with 84 million LTC compared to Bitcoin's 21 million.

While Litecoin is often used as a transfer of value similar to Bitcoin, its faster transaction speed makes it more suitable for everyday transactions. It has gained popularity among merchants and payment processors seeking an alternative to traditional payment systems.

Cardano is a third-generation blockchain platform that addresses the scalability, security, and sustainability challenges earlier cryptocurrencies face. Founded by Charles Hoskinson, one of the co-founders of Ethereum, Cardano emphasizes a research-driven approach to blockchain development.

The platform is designed to support the construction of DApps and smart contracts while focusing on sustainability and regulatory compliance. Cardano's blockchain utilizes a unique consensus mechanism called Ouroboros, which employs proof-of-stake principles for energy efficiency and scalability.

Cardano's team is actively working on enhancing the platform's functionalities, and it is split into separate layers, making upgrades and modifications more straightforward. This modular approach enables for greater flexibility and adaptability, which may contribute to the platform's long-term viability.

Dr. Gavin Wood, one of Ethereum's co-founders, founded the blockchain platform Polkadot. It aims to address the challenges of interoperability and scalability that isolated blockchain networks face. Polkadot's key innovation is its ability to connect multiple blockchains through its relay chain.

Polkadot's relay chain serves as a bridge, facilitating communication and data transfer between different blockchains or "parachains." This interoperability allows for exchanging assets and data across other networks, fostering a more connected and collaborative blockchain ecosystem.

The platform's design also focuses on scalability, as each parachain can process transactions independently, enhancing overall network efficiency. Polkadot's unique governance mechanism also allows stakeholders to propose and vote on network upgrades, enabling a more decentralized decision-making process.

Altcoins have evolved into a vast and diverse ecosystem, providing solutions and innovations that complement and extend beyond the original vision of Bitcoin. Ethereum has paved the way for smart contracts and DApps, enabling a wide range of decentralized applications and services. Ripple (XRP) seeks to revolutionize cross-border payments, making international remittances faster and more affordable.

Litecoin offers a faster transaction speed, positioning itself as a practical alternative for everyday transactions. Cardano, a third-generation blockchain, prioritizes research and sustainability to overcome scalability and security challenges. On the other hand, Polkadot focuses on interoperability, connecting various blockchains to create a more connected and collaborative ecosystem.

As the cryptocurrency landscape continues to evolve, altcoins will likely be crucial in driving technological advancements and addressing specific industry needs. These major altcoins and numerous others represent a dynamic space that will continue to shape the future of digital finance and decentralized applications. As new use cases and technological innovations emerge, the collective impact of altcoins is poised to expand the boundaries of blockchain technology and redefine the possibilities of decentralized digital currencies.

The broader impact of cryptocurrencies on finance and technology

Cryptocurrencies, led by the pioneering Bitcoin, have emerged as a disruptive force in the world of finance and technology. Since the creation of Bitcoin in 2009, the landscape of digital currencies has evolved rapidly, giving rise to a vast ecosystem of cryptocurrencies, blockchain technology, and decentralized finance (DeFi). This section explores the broader impact of cryptocurrencies on finance and technology, including their influence on traditional financial systems, the potential for financial inclusion, the rise of DeFi, and the challenges and opportunities they present for global economies.

Cryptocurrencies have sparked a paradigm shift in traditional finance. Historically, financial transactions relied on intermediaries like banks and payment processors to facilitate and validate transactions. With the advent of cryptocurrencies, financial interactions can occur directly between individuals, eliminating the need for intermediaries. This peer-to-peer aspect of cryptocurrencies fosters financial autonomy and empowers individuals with greater control over their assets.

Moreover, cryptocurrencies have challenged the concept of traditional currencies issued by central banks. Bitcoin's decentralized nature and capped supply have led some to view it as a potential alternative to fiat currencies and a hedge against inflation. Central banks have taken notice of this disruption and are exploring the development of central bank digital currencies (CBDCs) to modernize their monetary systems and maintain relevance in the digital era.

Cryptocurrencies can potentially bring financial services to the unbanked and underbanked populations globally. Traditional financial systems often exclude individuals without access to banking infrastructure or identification documents. In contrast, cryptocurrencies can be accessed with just a smartphone and an internet connection, making them more accessible to an extensive range of individuals.

In regions with limited banking services, cryptocurrencies offer a lifeline for remittances and cross-border transactions. Sending and receiving cryptocurrencies can bypass expensive and time-consuming intermediaries, reducing transaction costs and settlement times for remittance recipients.

The advent of cryptocurrencies has paved the way for the rise of DeFi, a new financial system built on blockchain technology and smart contracts. DeFi platforms provide decentralized alternatives to traditional financial services, such as lending, borrowing, trading, and yield farming.

These platforms operate without intermediaries, utilizing smart contracts to automate financial agreements and transactions. DeFi has attracted significant attention and investment, with its total value locked (TVL) in DeFi protocols reaching billions of dollars. The growing DeFi ecosystem promises to democratize finance, provide open access to financial services, and enable innovative financial products and services.

While cryptocurrencies offer numerous opportunities, they also present challenges for global economies. One of the primary concerns is the potential for increased financial crime and fraud. Cryptocurrencies' pseudonymous nature has attracted illicit activities, such as money laundering, ransomware attacks, and illegal transactions on the dark web. Regulators and law enforcement agencies are grappling with balancing fostering innovation and protecting consumers from criminal activities.

Additionally, the extreme volatility of cryptocurrency prices has raised concerns about investor protection and market stability. Sudden price fluctuations can lead to major losses for investors, especially those lacking experience or understanding of the crypto market. Regulatory frameworks are still evolving, with some countries embracing cryptocurrencies while others impose stringent restrictions or outright bans.

The development of cryptocurrencies has accelerated technological advancements in the fields of blockchain, cryptography, and decentralized systems. Blockchain, the underlying technology of most cryptocurrencies, has demonstrated its potential beyond financial applications. Its immutability, transparency, and decentralized nature have attracted interest from various sectors, such as supply chain management, healthcare, and voting systems.

Furthermore, the emergence of cryptocurrencies has sparked innovation in the realm of digital assets. Non-fungible tokens (NFTs) have gained traction as unique digital assets representing art, music, collectibles, and virtual real estate ownership. NFTs have opened new avenues for creators and artists to monetize their work directly, without intermediaries.

Cryptocurrencies, particularly those using the energy-intensive proof-of-work consensus mechanism, have been scrutinized for their environmental impact. The mining process entails solving complex mathematical puzzles and consumes vast amounts of electricity. Concerns have been raised about the carbon footprint of cryptocurrencies and their contribution to climate change.

In response to environmental concerns, some cryptocurrencies are exploring alternative consensus mechanisms, such as proof-of-stake, which require significantly less energy. Additionally, there is a growing push for sustainable mining practices and renewable energy sources to power cryptocurrency mining operations.

In conclusion, the broader impact of cryptocurrencies on finance and technology is multidimensional, with the potential to revolutionize traditional financial systems, drive innovation, and foster financial inclusion. The ongoing evolution of cryptocurrencies will undoubtedly shape the future of finance and technology, presenting both opportunities and challenges for global economies and societies. As the space continues to mature, responsible development, regulatory frameworks, and sustainable practices will be critical to maximizing the positive impact of cryptocurrencies on the global economy and technology landscape.

Chapter XI
Security and Risks in the Bitcoin Space

Common security threats for Bitcoin users

With the growing acceptance of Bitcoin and other cryptocurrencies, strong security measures are becoming more and more important. Cryptocurrencies operate on decentralized blockchain networks, providing users with financial sovereignty and privacy. However, this decentralization also exposes users to various security threats. This section explores the common security threats faced by Bitcoin users, including hacking attacks, phishing scams, malware, social engineering, and the risks associated with storing cryptocurrencies in online exchanges.

Hacking attacks targeting cryptocurrency users and platforms have been a significant concern in crypto. Hackers exploit vulnerabilities in exchanges, wallets, and individual accounts to steal digital assets. Notable hacking incidents have resulted in the loss of Bitcoin and other cryptocurrencies that is worth millions of dollars.

One common hacking method is the use of sophisticated malware, such as keyloggers and remote access Trojans, to gain unauthorized access to users' private keys or login credentials. Another technique involves targeting cryptocurrency exchanges and wallets that store large amounts of funds. Once hackers breach these platforms, they can transfer the stolen funds to their own wallets, making it challenging to trace and recover the stolen assets.

To mitigate hacking risks, users are advised to employ strong security practices, including the use of hardware wallets, multi-factor authentication (MFA), and regularly updating software and antivirus programs.

Phishing scams are prevalent in cryptocurrency, where malicious actors create fraudulent websites and emails that mimic legitimate platforms to deceive users into disclosing sensitive information. In the context of Bitcoin, phishing scams often target users' private keys, seed phrases, or login credentials.

Phishers may distribute fake emails claiming to be from cryptocurrency exchanges or wallet providers, requesting users to confirm their account information or reset their passwords. Unsuspecting users who fall victim to these scams inadvertently expose their private keys or passwords to attackers, leading to potential theft of their digital assets.

Users should practice caution when clicking on links in unsolicited emails or messages to avoid falling victim to phishing scams. Always verify the authenticity of the website or platform and never share sensitive information through unsecured channels.

Malware targeting cryptocurrency users is on the rise, and it comes in various forms, such as ransomware, cryptojacking, and clipboard hijacking. Ransomware attacks involve encrypting the victim's files and demanding a ransom or payment in Bitcoin or other cryptocurrencies for decryption. Cryptojacking, on the other hand, involves hackers using victims' devices to mine cryptocurrencies without their consent, draining computing resources and potentially damaging hardware.

Clipboard hijacking is another concerning malware that monitors users' clipboard activity, replacing legitimate cryptocurrency wallet addresses with those controlled by attackers. When users attempt to make transactions, they unknowingly send funds to the attackers instead of the intended recipient.

To mitigate malware risks, users should regularly update their operating systems and use reputable antivirus software. Malware infections can also be avoided by exercising caution while downloading files or accessing links from unreliable sources.

Social engineering attacks rely on psychological manipulation to deceive users into disclosing sensitive information or performing actions that compromising their security. These attacks exploit human vulnerabilities, such as trust and curiosity, to gain unauthorized access to users' cryptocurrency holdings.

One common social engineering tactic is impersonating customer support representatives or prominent figures in the cryptocurrency community to gain users' trust. Attackers may engage users in conversation through social media or email, convincing them to share private keys or seed phrases under the pretext of resolving an issue or offering investment opportunities.

To guard against social engineering attacks, users should be cautious when interacting with unknown individuals online and should verify the identity of anyone claiming to be associated with a cryptocurrency platform or service.

Storing cryptocurrencies on online exchanges poses inherent risks as third-party custodians hold users' assets. While reputable exchanges implement security measures, they can still be susceptible to hacking attacks and internal security breaches.

Cryptocurrency exchange hacks have resulted in substantial losses for users, prompting them to consider self-custody options, such as hardware wallets or software wallets where they have sole control over their private keys.

It is crucial for users to research and choose reputable exchanges with robust security practices and to avoid keeping large amounts of cryptocurrencies on exchanges for an extended period.

As the adoption of Bitcoin and cryptocurrencies continues to grow, so do the security threats faced by users. Hacking attacks, phishing scams, malware, social engineering, and the risks associated with storing assets on online exchanges are common security challenges in the crypto space.

To safeguard their holdings, users must prioritize security best practices, such as using hardware wallets, enabling multi-factor authentication, and remaining vigilant against phishing attempts. Staying informed about emerging threats and employing robust security measures will help users navigate the evolving landscape of cryptocurrency security and protect their digital assets from malicious actors. As the cryptocurrency ecosystem matures, collaboration between users, exchanges, and security experts will be essential in creating a safer environment for all participants.

Best practices for securing your Bitcoin holdings

With the increasing popularity and value of Bitcoin, ensuring the security of your digital assets has become paramount. As a decentralized and immutable digital currency, Bitcoin offers financial sovereignty, but it also places the responsibility of safeguarding your holdings solely on you, the user. This section explores the best practices for securing your Bitcoin holdings, covering topics such as choosing the right wallet, implementing strong passwords and authentication methods, utilizing hardware wallets, practicing safe online behavior, and staying informed about emerging threats.

The first step in securing your Bitcoin holdings is selecting the right wallet. Bitcoin wallets come in various forms, each with its own security features and trade-offs. The two main categories of wallets are hardware wallets and software wallets. Hardware wallets, or cold wallets, are tangible devices designed to store your private keys offline. These wallets provide an added layer of security as they are not connected to the internet when not in use, reducing the risk of remote hacking attacks. Popular hardware wallets include Ledger Nano S, Trezor, and KeepKey. Purchasing hardware wallets directly from reputable sources is essential to avoid the risk of receiving tampered devices.

On the other hand, software wallets can be classified into desktop wallets, mobile wallets, and web wallets. Desktop wallets are downloaded on your computer, mobile wallets on your smartphone, and web wallets are accessible through a web browser. While software wallets offer convenience, they are more vulnerable to online threats than hardware wallets. It is advisable to use hardware wallets for storing significant amounts of Bitcoin and software wallets for day-to-day transactions with smaller amounts.

Securing your Bitcoin holdings starts with the basics of password management. Generate a unique and robust passwords for all your accounts and wallets, ensuring they are not easily guessable. Avoid using personal information or common phrases in your passwords, and consider using a combination of the letters in uppercase and lowercase, numbers, and special characters. Additionally, enable multi-factor authentication (MFA) whenever possible. MFA necessitates users to provide two or more forms of identification before accessing an account, making it significantly harder for unauthorized individuals to acquire access. Using biometric authentication, like facial recognition or fingerprint, on your mobile wallets or hardware wallets can also add a further layer of security.

As mentioned earlier, hardware wallets offer the highest level of security for your Bitcoin holdings. These devices store your private keys offline, keeping them away from potential online threats. Even if your computer or smartphone is compromised, a hardware wallet's private keys remain secure within the device. When setting up your hardware wallet for the first time, it generates a recovery seed, a series of words that act as a backup for your private keys.

Ensure you store this seed phrase securely, preferably in multiple physical locations and away from prying eyes. Losing access to your recovery seed could result in the permanent loss of your Bitcoin holdings.

Malware targeting cryptocurrency users is on the rise, and it comes in various forms, such as ransomware, cryptojacking, and clipboard hijacking. Ransomware attacks involve encrypting the victim's files and demanding a ransom or payment in Bitcoin or other cryptocurrencies for decryption. Cryptojacking involves hackers using victims' devices to mine cryptocurrencies without their consent, draining computing resources and potentially damaging hardware. Clipboard hijacking is another concerning malware that monitors users' clipboard activity, replacing legitimate cryptocurrency wallet addresses with those controlled by attackers. When users attempt to make transactions, they unknowingly send funds to the attackers instead of the intended recipient.

To mitigate malware risks, users should regularly update their operating systems and use reputable antivirus software. Malware infections can also be avoided by exercising caution while downloading files or accessing links from unreliable sources.

Social engineering attacks rely on psychological manipulation to deceive users into disclosing sensitive information or performing actions compromising their security. These attacks exploit human vulnerabilities, such as trust and curiosity, to gain unauthorized access to users' cryptocurrency holdings. One common social engineering tactic is impersonating customer support representatives or prominent figures in the cryptocurrency community to gain users' trust. Attackers may engage users in conversation through social media or email, convincing them to share private keys or seed phrases under the pretext of resolving an issue or offering investment opportunities.

To guard against social engineering attacks, users should be cautious when interacting with unknown individuals online and should verify the identity of anyone claiming to be associated with a cryptocurrency platform or service.

Storing cryptocurrencies on online exchanges poses inherent risks as third-party custodians hold users' assets. While reputable exchanges implement security measures, they can still be susceptible to hacking attacks and internal security breaches. Cryptocurrency exchange hacks have resulted in substantial losses for users, prompting them to consider self-custody options, such as hardware wallets or software wallets where they have sole control over their private keys. It is crucial for users to research and choose reputable exchanges with robust security practices and to avoid keeping large amounts of cryptocurrencies on exchanges for an extended period.

Securing your Bitcoin holdings requires a combination of best practices and vigilance. By choosing the right wallet, implementing strong passwords and authentication methods, utilizing hardware wallets, practicing safe online behavior, and staying informed about emerging threats, you can significantly mitigate the risk of falling victim to security breaches. Remember that safeguarding your

Bitcoin holdings is ultimately your responsibility. Take the necessary precautions, stay educated about security risks, and remain proactive in implementing security measures to protect your digital assets. In a constantly evolving landscape, being proactive and diligent will go a long way in keeping your Bitcoin holdings safe and secure.

Major Bitcoin-related hacks and their lessons

As Bitcoin's popularity and value have soared, it has become a prime target for hackers seeking to take advantage of the vulnerabilities and gain unauthorized access to users' funds and sensitive information. Over the years, several high-profile Bitcoin-related hacks have resulted in significant losses in terms of monetary value and user trust. This section explores some of the major Bitcoin-related hacks that have occurred and the valuable lessons they have taught the cryptocurrency community about security, vigilance, and the importance of safeguarding digital assets.

Mt. Gox (2011 - 2014)

One of the most infamous Bitcoin-related hacks was the Mt. Gox incident, which took place between 2011 and 2014. Mt. Gox, a Japan-based Bitcoin exchange, was once the world's largest platform for purchasing and selling Bitcoin. However, poor security practices and a lack of proper auditing allowed hackers to exploit the exchange's system vulnerabilities.

The Mt. Gox hack resulted in the loss of approximately 850,000 Bitcoins, worth billions of dollars at the time. The hack sent shockwaves through the cryptocurrency community, leading to widespread panic and a significant decline in Bitcoin's price. It also highlighted the risks of leaving large amounts of funds on centralized exchanges.

Lesson Learned: The Mt. Gox hack emphasized the importance of using reputable and secure exchanges for trading and storing cryptocurrencies. It highlighted the need for exchanges to implement robust security measures, conduct regular audits, and segregate user funds to prevent large-scale losses.

Bitfinex (2016)

In 2016, Bitfinex, another prominent cryptocurrency exchange, suffered a major breach in security leading to the loss of approximately 120,000 Bitcoins. The hackers exploited vulnerabilities in Bitfinex's multi-signature wallet setup, a security feature meant to provide an extra layer of protection.

The hack raised questions about the security of multi-signature wallets and emphasized the need for continuous monitoring and improvement of security protocols.

Lesson Learned: The Bitfinex hack underscored the importance of regularly auditing and stress-testing security measures, even if they are considered advanced or cutting-edge. It also highlighted the need for transparent communication with users during and after a security breach, helping to rebuild trust in the platform.

NiceHash (2017)

In 2017, NiceHash, a popular mining marketplace, experienced a significant breach in security , resulting in the loss of approximately 4,700 Bitcoins from users' wallets. The hackers exploited weaknesses in NiceHash's payment system, allowing them to transfer the stolen funds to their own wallet.

The incident affected the platform and individual miners who had entrusted their mining rewards to the service.

Lesson Learned: The NiceHash hack emphasized the importance of secure payment systems and the need for platforms that handle user funds to have strong security protocols in place. It also reminded users to consider the risks associated with third-party services, even in the mining sector.

Binance (2019)

In 2019, Binance, one of the world's largest cryptocurrency exchanges, experienced a major security breach that led to the theft of approximately 7,000 Bitcoins. The hackers employed various techniques, including phishing and malware attacks, to gain access to users' two-factor authentication codes and API keys.

Binance quickly responded to the breach by halting trading and withdrawals, and it later reimbursed affected users from its Secure Asset Fund for Users (SAFU).

Lesson Learned: The Binance hack highlighted the importance of educating users about the risks of phishing scams and malware attacks. It also demonstrated the value of exchange-reserved funds, such as SAFU, to compensate users for potential losses.

Twitter Hack (2020)

In July 2020, a large-scale Twitter hack targeted several high-profile accounts, like Elon Musk, Barack Obama, and Bill Gates. The hackers used social engineering tactics to access Twitter's internal tools and post fraudulent messages promoting a Bitcoin scam.

Although the hack did not directly involve stealing Bitcoin, it raised concerns about the security of social media platforms and the potential for cryptocurrency scams.

Lesson Learned: The Twitter hack served as a reminder of the risks associated with centralized platforms and the need for robust security measures in social media companies. It also highlighted the importance of verifying information independently and being cautious about offers that seem too good to be true.

Poly Network (2021)

In August 2021, Poly Network, a cross-chain decentralized finance (DeFi) platform, suffered a massive hack leading to the loss of over $600 million worth of various cryptocurrencies, including Bitcoin. The hacker exploited a vulnerability in Poly Network's smart contract code, allowing them to transfer the stolen funds to their own addresses.

The Poly Network hack was unique in that the hacker eventually returned most of the stolen funds, claiming to have done it for fun and to expose weaknesses in the platform's security.

Lesson Learned: The Poly Network hack demonstrated the need for thorough security audits of smart contracts and the importance of bug bounty programs to incentivize white-hat hackers to identify vulnerabilities before malicious actors do.

The major Bitcoin-related hacks that have occurred over the years serve as stark reminders of the ever-present security risks in the cryptocurrency space. They highlight the importance of choosing reputable and secure platforms for trading and storing cryptocurrencies and the need for continuous improvement and auditing of security protocols. Centralized exchanges, in particular, have been frequent targets of hackers, emphasizing the need for users to exercise caution and consider self-custody options such as hardware wallets.

Additionally, the hacks underscore the value of transparency and timely communication with users during and after a security breach, as this can help rebuild trust in affected platforms. Education and awareness about security risks, including phishing scams and malware attacks, are also crucial for users to protect their digital assets effectively.

Furthermore, the importance of secure smart contract coding and vulnerability testing cannot be overstated, especially in the context of decentralized finance and blockchain-based applications.

As the cryptocurrency ecosystem evolves, security practices will play a central role in guaranteeing the long-term success and adoption of digital assets like Bitcoin. The lessons learned from these major hacks provide valuable insights into how the community can collectively work to strengthen the security infrastructure and protect users' assets worldwide. The cryptocurrency space can move towards a more secure and resilient future through a combination of best practices, vigilance, and continued innovation.

Chapter XII
The Future of Bitcoin

Scaling solutions and the Lightning Network

As the popularity of Bitcoin has grown, so needs to address its scalability limitations. The Bitcoin network's ability to process transactions is constrained by its block size and block time, resulting in occasional congestion and high fees during periods of increased activity. Several scaling solutions have been proposed and implemented to overcome these challenges and facilitate a higher transaction throughput. One of the most promising solutions is the Lightning Network. This section explores the various scaling solutions for Bitcoin and delves into the Lightning Network's mechanics, advantages, and challenges.

The need for scaling solutions arose as Bitcoin's original design intended it to be a peer-to-peer electronic cash system, enabling fast and low-cost transactions without intermediaries. However, as adoption grew, the network faced congestion during peak usage, causing transaction confirmation times to increase and fees to rise significantly. This situation challenged Bitcoin's usability for everyday transactions and highlighted the necessity for scaling solutions.

On-chain scaling solutions aim to increase the transaction throughput by directly modifying the Bitcoin network's underlying protocols. One such solution was the block size increase, which led to a contentious debate within the community. Advocates argued that increasing the block size would accommodate more transactions per block, thereby reducing fees and processing times. However, opponents raised concerns about the potential centralization of mining power and increased storage requirements for running a full node. In 2017, a hard fork led to the creation of Bitcoin Cash, which implemented an increased block size of 8 MB. Nevertheless, the scaling debate remained divisive, and the Bitcoin community explored other approaches to address scalability without compromising on decentralization.

Segregated Witness, often abbreviated as SegWit, was implemented in August 2017 as a soft fork upgrade to the Bitcoin protocol. It separated the transaction data (witness) from the transaction signature, including more transaction information in each block. This effectively increased the block's capacity, enabling more transactions without directly increasing the block size. SegWit's adoption gradually increased, leading to a reduction in transaction fees and improved scalability. It also paved the way for implementing more advanced scaling solutions like the Lightning Network.

By establishing payment channels off-chain, the Lightning Network serves as a layer-two scaling solution that makes quick and affordable micropayments possible. In 2015, Joseph Poon and Thaddeus Dryja put forth the idea in their whitepaper titled "The

Bitcoin Lightning Network: Scalable Off-Chain Instant Payments." The Lightning Network creates payment channels between users, allowing them to conduct multiple transactions without the need to broadcast each one to the Bitcoin blockchain. These channels are set up using multi-signature addresses, and the participants commit a certain amount of Bitcoin to the channel's balance. Users can send and receive Bitcoin between themselves instantaneously and for a little fee once the channel is open. The transactions are only recorded on the Bitcoin blockchain when the channel is closed, aggregating multiple transactions into a single on-chain transaction.

The Lightning Network offers several advantages for Bitcoin users and the overall network. First, it greatly enhances scalability by enabling off-chain transactions, potentially processing thousands of transactions per second, a vast improvement over the current on-chain throughput. Second, Lightning transactions are nearly instant, making them ideal for everyday micropayments and seamlessly enabling use cases like buying coffee or paying for online content. Third, users benefit from lower fees, as transactions on the Lightning Network are significantly cheaper than those processed on-chain during periods of network congestion. Fourth, with most transactions occurring off-chain, the demand for block space is reduced, leading to a less congested Bitcoin blockchain and lower fees for those who still prefer on-chain transactions. Finally, the Lightning Network has been explored for use with other blockchains, allowing for potential interoperability and cross-chain transactions.

Despite its promising advantages, the Lightning Network also faces challenges and limitations. Network routing complexity is one of the challenges, as the Lightning Network's success depends on a robust network of well-connected nodes. Routing payments through intermediaries may become more complex as the network grows, potentially affecting transaction success rates. Another challenge is channel liquidity management. Users must have sufficient liquidity in their payment channels to make payments on the Lightning Network. Managing channel liquidity effectively can be challenging, especially for nodes with limited funds. Security concerns also arise as the Lightning Network is an emerging technology. While the underlying Bitcoin protocol is battle-tested, the Lightning Network introduces additional complexities and potential vulnerabilities. As the network grows, it becomes crucial to maintain robust security measures to protect users and their funds. Moreover, depending on the distribution of nodes and payment channel relationships, the Lightning Network could become more centralized over time. Large and well-connected nodes may gain more influence and control over the network, which could raise concerns about decentralization. The Lightning Network may also introduce privacy challenges, as transaction information is shared between participating nodes. While efforts have been made to address privacy concerns, users must remain vigilant about their data and transaction privacy.

Despite these challenges, the Lightning Network has grown steadily since its inception. As developers and the community continue to improve the technology and address its limitations, the Lightning

Network's adoption and utility are expected to increase. The network's success relies on a robust network of well-connected nodes and ongoing innovation to address security and scalability challenges.

In conclusion, scaling solutions like the Lightning Network are essential for Bitcoin's continued growth and broader adoption. The development and implementation of these solutions reflect the cryptocurrency community's commitment to addressing the challenges associated with scaling while preserving the core principles of decentralization and security. As the Lightning Network evolves and overcomes its limitations, it holds the potential to transform Bitcoin into a more efficient, scalable, and widely accepted means of payment and value transfer. However, users and developers must remain vigilant in addressing security concerns and ensuring that these solutions enhance, rather than compromise, the integrity of the Bitcoin network. Through collaborative efforts and ongoing research, the Bitcoin community can continue to enhance the scalability and efficiency of the network, fostering its long-term success as a revolutionary digital currency.

Potential challenges and opportunities

Since its inception in 2009, Bitcoin—the first and most well-known cryptocurrency—has made a tremendous impact on the technology and finance industries. As it continues gaining traction and adoption, it faces challenges and opportunities that shape its future trajectory. This section explores the potential challenges Bitcoin may encounter and the opportunities it can seize to cement its position as a transformative force in the global financial landscape.

The first significant challenge facing Bitcoin is the ever-evolving regulatory landscape. As a decentralized and borderless digital asset, Bitcoin operates outside traditional financial systems, making it challenging for regulators to establish comprehensive frameworks. Countries have taken varied approaches to regulate cryptocurrencies, from outright bans to embracing them as legitimate financial instruments. Navigating these differing regulatory environments poses challenges for users, businesses, and exchanges operating in multiple jurisdictions. Overly restrictive regulations could stifle innovation and hinder mainstream adoption, while lax regulations might expose users to potential risks, such as scams and fraudulent schemes.

However, this challenge also allows Bitcoin to engage in constructive dialogue with regulators and policymakers. Collaborating with regulators can lead to more balanced and effective regulations that promote innovation, protect consumers, and ensure financial stability. Additionally, clearer regulations can instill confidence in institutional investors and pave the way for increased participation in the cryptocurrency space.

Another challenge for Bitcoin is scalability and network efficiency. Bitcoin's original design limits its transaction processing capacity, leading to congestion during periods of high demand. Scaling solutions, such as Segregated Witness (SegWit) and the Lightning Network, have been implemented to address this challenge.

However, continued growth in adoption may necessitate further scaling innovations. Maintaining a balance between transaction throughput and network efficiency is crucial to ensure Bitcoin's competitiveness as a payment system. Scalability challenges can lead to higher transaction fees and longer confirmation times, potentially hindering its use for everyday transactions.

Nonetheless, this challenge also opens up an opportunity for continued research and development of innovative scaling solutions. Collaboration among developers and stakeholders can foster the implementation of efficient, secure, and decentralized scaling solutions that enhance Bitcoin's network efficiency and improve its utility as a medium of exchange.

Another challenge that Bitcoin faces is its energy consumption and environmental impact. Bitcoin's proof-of-work consensus mechanism requires substantial computational power, leading to significant energy consumption. Critics argue that this energy-intensive process contributes to environmental concerns, particularly regarding carbon emissions from power-hungry mining operations. While some miners have explored renewable energy sources to reduce their carbon footprint, addressing the environmental impact of Bitcoin mining remains a challenge.

However, this challenge also allows Bitcoin to advance towards more energy-efficient consensus mechanisms, such as proof-of-stake. Embracing such mechanisms could mitigate Bitcoin's environmental impact and align the cryptocurrency with the growing global focus on sustainability. Furthermore, promoting the use of renewable energy sources for mining operations can contribute to a greener and more sustainable Bitcoin network.

Financial inclusion and access represent another challenge for Bitcoin. While its decentralized nature empowers individuals to control their finances, certain barriers still hinder its accessibility to all. Technological literacy, internet connectivity, and access to digital wallets can present challenges for individuals in underserved regions. Addressing the issue of financial inclusion through educational initiatives, user-friendly interfaces, and increased connectivity can unlock the potential of Bitcoin for millions of unbanked or underbanked individuals worldwide.

Nonetheless, this challenge also allows Bitcoin to forge partnerships with non-governmental organizations and financial institutions. Collaborating with such organizations can foster financial education and improve access to cryptocurrencies for underserved communities. Developing mobile-friendly wallets and solutions tailored to low-bandwidth environments can also promote greater inclusivity.

Security and custodial risks are significant challenges for Bitcoin. As a bearer asset, Bitcoin requires users to safeguard their private keys diligently. Loss of private keys can result in irreversible loss of funds, and the irrecoverable nature of transactions poses risks for those unfamiliar with the technology. Additionally, while self-custody provides enhanced security, it also places the responsibility entirely on the user. In contrast, custodial services introduce the risk of third-party hacks and mismanagement.

However, this challenge also allows Bitcoin to improve user education on best security practices. Using hardware wallets can enhance individual security and reduce the risks associated with self-custody. Furthermore, collaboration between hardware wallet manufacturers and exchanges can facilitate secure, seamless user experiences and mitigate custodial risks.

Volatility and price fluctuations represent another significant challenge for Bitcoin. Its price volatility has been a defining characteristic since its inception. While it has attracted investors seeking high returns, sudden price swings can lead to concerns about its use as a stable store of value and medium of exchange. Volatility poses challenges for merchants and businesses in pricing their goods and services, potentially deterring them from accepting Bitcoin as a payment method.

However, this challenge also allows Bitcoin to mature as a financial instrument. As its market matures and adoption increases, price volatility may decrease. Developing stablecoins and payment processors that offer instant conversion from Bitcoin to fiat currencies can also mitigate volatility-related concerns for merchants and consumers.

Integration with traditional finance represents another challenge for Bitcoin. As it gains recognition and acceptance, it becomes crucial to close the gap between the traditional financial system and the cryptocurrency space. While some institutions have embraced Bitcoin, others remain hesitant due to concerns about its regulatory status, security, and volatility.

However, this challenge also allows Bitcoin to foster greater acceptance and use. Collaborative efforts between cryptocurrency companies and traditional financial institutions can create a bridge for seamless integration. Addressing concerns about regulatory compliance, security standards, and the benefits of cryptocurrencies can also contribute to greater acceptance.

Privacy and regulatory compliance represent another challenge for Bitcoin. Its transparent nature enables public access to all transaction details on the blockchain. While this feature enhances transparency and auditability, it can raise privacy concerns for individuals who wish to conduct transactions discreetly. However, ensuring compliance with anti-money laundering (AML) and know-your-customer (KYC) regulations can pose challenges due to the pseudonymous nature of Bitcoin transactions.

This challenge presents an opportunity for Bitcoin to balance privacy and regulatory compliance. Research and development of privacy-focused solutions, such as confidential transactions and zero-knowledge proofs, can enhance transaction privacy while still complying with regulatory requirements. Furthermore, striving for transparency and clear communication with regulators can foster a cooperative relationship and contribute to a more inclusive financial ecosystem.

In conclusion, Bitcoin's journey is marked by potential challenges and opportunities. As the world's first cryptocurrency, it has laid the foundation for a decentralized financial revolution. However, its success is contingent upon addressing challenges related to regulation, scalability, energy consumption, financial inclusion, security, volatility, integration with traditional finance, and privacy. Embracing these difficulties as opportunities for growth and improvement can position Bitcoin as a transformative force in the global financial landscape. By fostering collaboration, innovation, and an unwavering commitment to the principles of decentralization and financial empowerment, Bitcoin can continue to shape the future of finance, transcending borders and empowering individuals worldwide. As it navigates the evolving landscape, Bitcoin remains a symbol of hope and resilience, a digital currency that challenges the status quo and heralds a new era of financial freedom.

How Bitcoin might integrate into the mainstream economy

Since its launch in 2009, Bitcoin, the very first and most widely recognized cryptocurrency, has seen significant development. Initially regarded as a niche and experimental digital currency, it has now evolved into a global phenomenon with a market capitalization in the trillions of dollars. As Bitcoin's popularity grows, questions arise about its potential integration into the mainstream economy. This section explores the possibilities and challenges of how Bitcoin might seamlessly integrate into the global financial system, transforming how we perceive and interact with money.

One of the primary hurdles that Bitcoin must overcome to achieve mainstream integration is regulatory clarity and legal recognition. Different countries have taken varied approaches to cryptocurrency regulation, leading to a fragmented landscape. Some nations have embraced Bitcoin and other cryptocurrencies, recognizing them as legal financial instruments, while others remain cautious or have imposed outright bans. The lack of standardized regulations can create uncertainty for businesses and users, potentially hindering broader adoption.

To integrate into the mainstream economy, Bitcoin needs more precise and more consistent regulatory frameworks that provide legal certainty. Collaborating with governments and financial regulatory bodies to establish guidelines for using and taxation cryptocurrencies can promote investor confidence and attract institutional interest. Legal recognition can also encourage traditional financial institutions to offer cryptocurrency-related services, such as custodial solutions and investment products, to their clients.

For Bitcoin to become a significant player in the mainstream economy, it needs widespread institutional adoption. The involvement of large financial institutions, such as banks and asset management firms, can bring liquidity, credibility, and stability to the cryptocurrency market. Institutional investors often have significant capital to deploy, which could contribute to reducing Bitcoin's price volatility.

To attract institutional investors, Bitcoin needs robust infrastructure and regulatory-compliant platforms. Developing secure custodial solutions, regulated cryptocurrency exchanges, and investment vehicles, such as exchange-traded funds (ETFs), can facilitate institutional participation. Furthermore, integrating Bitcoin into existing financial systems, such as payment processors and wealth management platforms, can make it more accessible to a broader audience.

Bitcoin must become a viable payment system for everyday transactions to integrate into the mainstream economy. Currently, Bitcoin faces challenges such as slow transaction confirmation times and high fees during periods of network congestion. These issues can hinder its use for small-value transactions, like purchasing a cup of coffee or paying for goods online.

To address these challenges, second-layer scaling solutions like the Lightning Network can provide faster and cheaper transactions, making micro-payments feasible on the Bitcoin network. Collaborations between Bitcoin wallet providers, payment processors, and merchants can create a seamless user payment experience, encouraging broader adoption.

Bitcoin's borderless nature opens up opportunities for cross-border payments and financial inclusion. In regions with insufficient access to traditional banking services, Bitcoin can offer a viable alternative for transferring funds and conducting financial transactions. Its decentralized nature allows individuals to control their finances without relying on intermediary institutions.

To leverage this potential, Bitcoin needs user-friendly wallets and easy-to-use interfaces that cater to diverse user demographics. Furthermore, partnerships with remittance companies and money transfer services can facilitate cross-border transactions at lower costs and faster speeds than traditional methods.

As a store of value, Bitcoin has gained recognition as a potential hedge against inflation and economic uncertainty. Unlike fiat currencies, Bitcoin's supply is limited, with a predetermined maximum of 21 million coins. This scarcity feature appeals to investors seeking a safe haven asset during economic turbulence.

Bitcoin needs to maintain its long-term price stability and resilience to strengthen its position as a store of value. Building trust among investors and the general public through transparent and secure infrastructure can enhance its perception as a reliable store of wealth.

To integrate fully into the mainstream economy, Bitcoin must extend its reach beyond a standalone digital currency. Integrating Bitcoin with other financial services, such as lending, borrowing, and insurance, can create a comprehensive financial ecosystem.

Collateralized loans and decentralized lending platforms can offer new financial opportunities for Bitcoin holders. Smart contracts on blockchain platforms can enable secure insurance services without intermediaries. DeFi (Decentralized Finance) protocols can expand the utility of Bitcoin, allowing users to access a wide range of financial goods and services directly from their digital wallets.

Public education and awareness are essential factors in Bitcoin's integration into the mainstream economy. Misconceptions and misinformation about cryptocurrencies can deter potential users and investors. Educating the public about the benefits and risks of Bitcoin can foster a more informed and receptive audience.

Raising awareness can include media campaigns, educational materials, and partnerships with educational institutions. Governments and financial regulators can also play a role in educating the public about responsible cryptocurrency usage and the importance of financial literacy.

As Bitcoin gains prominence, concerns about its environmental impact have surfaced. The energy-intensive nature of proof-of-work mining has drawn criticism for its carbon footprint. Bitcoin must address these environmental concerns and adopt more sustainable mining practices to integrate into the mainstream economy.

Transitioning to renewable energy sources for mining operations and exploring alternative consensus mechanisms, such as proof-of-stake, can reduce Bitcoin's environmental impact. Emphasizing eco-friendly initiatives can also resonate with socially responsible investors and institutions.

In conclusion, Bitcoin's journey into the mainstream economy presents both challenges and opportunities. Regulatory clarity, institutional adoption, payment system improvements, financial inclusion, and integration with traditional financial services are key factors in its successful integration. Educating the public about Bitcoin's potential and addressing environmental concerns will also play a critical role.

As Bitcoin evolves and overcomes these challenges, it has the capacity to revolutionize the global financial landscape. By leveraging its unique features, such as decentralization, borderlessness, and scarcity, Bitcoin can provide an alternative financial system that empowers individuals and fosters economic inclusivity. Through collaboration, innovation, and responsible stewardship, Bitcoin may pave the way for a more decentralized, equitable, and interconnected financial future.

Conclusion

Recap of Bitcoin's revolutionary potential

The first and most well-known cryptocurrency, Bitcoin emerged in 2009 as a radical and disruptive innovation. Over the years, it has garnered global attention and sparked debates about its potential impact on the world of finance and beyond. This section recaps Bitcoin's revolutionary potential and its transformative role in reshaping the financial landscape and society at large.

At the heart of Bitcoin's revolutionary potential lies its decentralized nature. Unlike traditional financial systems controlled by central authorities, Bitcoin operates on a peer-to-peer network, where every participant has equal rights and responsibilities. This decentralization grants financial empowerment to individuals, as they gain control over their funds without relying on intermediary institutions. By removing the need for third-party intermediaries, Bitcoin challenges the traditional banking model and offers a more inclusive and accessible financial ecosystem.

Bitcoin's borderless nature allows for frictionless cross-border transactions. Traditional remittance processes are often slow, expensive, and fraught with intermediaries. With Bitcoin, individuals can send and receive funds across borders with greater speed and lower fees, promoting financial inclusion for the unbanked and also the underbanked populations. Moreover, in regions with limited access to traditional banking services, Bitcoin provides an alternative means of transacting and accumulating wealth, bridging the gap between developed and developing economies.

The concept of financial sovereignty is central to Bitcoin's revolutionary potential. Through Bitcoin's public-key cryptography, users can control their private keys, giving them complete ownership and control over their funds. This level of control and sovereignty was impossible with traditional banking systems, where banks and governments have authority over one's funds. Bitcoin empowers individuals to become their own bank, fostering a sense of ownership and responsibility over their financial assets.

In many countries, governments exercise strict control over financial transactions, leading to censorship and limitations on freedom of expression. Bitcoin's decentralized nature and cryptographic security provide censorship resistance, ensuring that any central authority cannot censor or control transactions. This feature makes Bitcoin a powerful tool for individuals in countries with restrictive financial regimes, allowing them to engage in unrestricted financial transactions and express their views without fear of censorship.

The Bitcoin blockchain offers a transparent and immutable ledger of all transactions ever conducted on the network. This transparency enhances auditability, as anyone can verify and trace transactions on the blockchain. Unlike traditional financial systems, where opaque transactions can lead to mistrust and uncertainty, Bitcoin's transparency promotes trust and accountability. This feature is particularly valuable for charities, businesses, and governments seeking to demonstrate the integrity of their financial operations.

As a store of value, Bitcoin has gained recognition as a potential hedge against inflation and economic uncertainty. Unlike fiat currencies, Bitcoin's supply is limited, with a predetermined maximum of 21 million coins. This scarcity feature appeals to investors seeking a safe haven asset during economic turbulence.

Bitcoin's revolutionary potential extends beyond its immediate impact on the financial landscape. As more people accept cryptocurrencies and blockchain technology, the traditional banking model may undergo significant disruption. Central banks and financial institutions are exploring the concept of central bank digital currencies (CBDCs) to compete with cryptocurrencies and harness blockchain's benefits.

Bitcoin's emergence has sparked a wave of innovation in finance and technology. The underlying blockchain technology has led to the development of numerous cryptocurrencies and decentralized applications (DApps) that offer unique use cases. Furthermore, the idea of smart contracts—made possible by blockchain technology—has created novel possibilities for programmable and automated financial arrangements.

While Bitcoin's revolutionary potential is undeniable, it also faces several challenges on its journey to mainstream adoption. Scalability, energy consumption, regulatory clarity, and security concerns are among the primary hurdles that must be addressed. Collaborative efforts from the cryptocurrency community, policymakers, and financial institutions are essential to unlocking Bitcoin's full potential.

In conclusion, Bitcoin's revolutionary potential is founded on its decentralized nature, borderless transactions, financial sovereignty, censorship resistance, transparency, and store of value attributes. It has sparked innovation, challenged traditional financial systems, and empowered individuals worldwide. As Bitcoin continues to evolve, its impact on finance and society will likely expand, fostering a future where financial freedom and empowerment are more accessible to all. The endless possibilities of cryptocurrencies and blockchain technology may be fully realized in a more inclusive and fair financial landscape that is made possible by acknowledging the opportunities and challenges that lie ahead. As the world grapples with economic uncertainties and technological advancements, Bitcoin stands at the forefront, offering a glimpse into the transformative power of decentralized digital currencies.

Final thoughts on the future of digital currencies

As we delve into the world of digital currencies, the future appears promising, yet uncertain. Cryptocurrencies, particularly Bitcoin, have ignited discussions about the future of money, finance, and the global economy. This section explores the final thoughts on the future of digital currencies, considering their potential impact on financial systems, technological innovation, and societal transformation.

At the heart of the future of digital currencies lies the evolution of financial systems. Digital currencies have the potential to revolutionize traditional financial systems. The centralized structure of traditional banking is challenged by the idea of decentralized and borderless transactions, opening the door for a more open and accessible financial environment. As the adoption of digital currencies grows, we may witness a transformation in how individuals store, transfer, and invest their money. Central banks and financial institutions are already exploring the notion of central bank digital currencies (or CBDCs) to harness the benefits of blockchain technology and enhance monetary policies.

Beyond digital currencies realm, blockchain technology stands as a transformative force. Its decentralized, immutable, and transparent nature finds applications beyond finance, in areas like supply chain management, healthcare, and voting systems. Blockchain's potential to revolutionize various industries highlights the versatility and impact of this groundbreaking technology. Blockchain technology and digital currencies will continue to interact in the future, paving the way for more effective, safe, and transparent systems.

The rise of digital currencies has sparked innovation in financial technology (FinTech). Developing smart contracts, decentralized finance (or DeFi) protocols, and non-fungible tokens (or NFTs) has opened up new possibilities for financial services and creative expression. Additionally, the concept of programmable money and automated financial agreements reshapes how we perceive and interact with financial transactions. As the FinTech landscape evolves, digital currencies will likely be instrumental in shaping the future of finance.

The future of digital currencies is closely linked to the regulatory environment. Governments and financial regulators are grappling with the challenges posed by cryptocurrencies, balancing the need for innovation with the risks of potential abuse. Balancing consumer protection, financial stability, and fostering innovation remains a delicate task. Clear and consistent regulations are essential to provide legal certainty for businesses and users, encouraging responsible growth in the digital currency space.

As digital currencies gain prominence, global adoption becomes critical in shaping their future. In developed economies, cryptocurrencies may serve as an investment asset or a store of value. However, in developing regions, they hold the potential to bridge financial inclusion gaps by providing access to financial services for the unbanked as well as the underbanked populations. Collaborative efforts between governments, businesses, and technology providers are crucial in expanding digital currency adoption worldwide.

The environmental impact of digital currencies, particularly Bitcoin, has drawn attention to the energy consumption of blockchain networks. As the demand for digital currencies rises, addressing sustainability concerns becomes imperative.

Technological advancements, such as the transition to proof-of-stake consensus mechanisms, can significantly reduce the carbon footprint of digital currency networks. Striving for eco-friendly practices is essential for ensuring the long-term viability of digital currencies in a world increasingly focused on environmental preservation.

The future of digital currencies extends beyond the realm of finance and technology. It carries societal implications that challenge established norms and systems. Concepts of financial sovereignty, censorship resistance, and individual ownership over money empower individuals to take control of their financial destinies. Additionally, adopting digital currencies may bring new opportunities for financial education, promoting financial literacy among users.

The future of digital currencies lies in the hands of collaboration and innovation. Blockchain technology and digital currencies are still in their nascent stages, leaving room for exploration, experimentation, and improvement. Collaborative efforts between governments, businesses, technology developers, and communities are vital to unlock the full potential of digital currencies. By fostering innovation, research, and open dialogue, we can shape a future that embraces the transformative power of digital currencies for the betterment of society.

In conclusion, the future of digital currencies is a tale of disruption, innovation, and global impact. As we navigate the uncharted waters of this digital revolution, the potential for financial empowerment, technological advancements, and societal transformation looms large. Digital currencies promise to reshape financial systems, promote financial inclusion, and revolutionize various industries through blockchain technology. However, the journey towards this future is not without challenges. Environmental concerns, regulatory considerations, and the need for sustainable and responsible growth require careful navigation.

As we approach this horizon, it becomes clear that the future of digital currencies will be shaped by collaboration, innovation, and the collective desire for a more inclusive and equitable financial landscape. Embracing the opportunities and challenges ahead, we venture into a world where digital currencies are symbols of financial freedom, technological progress, and the human potential for transformative change. Digital currencies of the future provide a blank canvas onto which we might draw the image of a more unified, capable, and resilient world community.

Thank you for buying and reading/listening to our book. If you found this book useful/helpful please take a few minutes and leave a review on the platform where you purchased our book. Your feedback matters greatly to us.